Loving & Leading from the Inside Out

Loving & Leading from the Inside Out

A GUIDE TO HEALING AND INSPIRED CHANGE

WENDE BIRTCH,
M.S., M.A., L.M.H.C.

EPIGRAPH BOOKS
RHINEBECK, NEW YORK

Loving and Leading from the Inside Out: A Guide to Healing and Inspired Change © Copyright 2018 by Wende Birtch, M.S., M.A., L.M.H.C.

All rights reserved. No part of this book may be used or reproduced in any manner except in critical articles or reviews. Contact the author for information.

ISBN 978-1-948796-49-1

Library of Congress Control Number 2018963701

Book design by Colin Rolfe

Epigraph Books
22 East Market Street, Suite 304
Rhinebeck, NY 12572
(845) 876-4861
www.EpigraphPS.com

Table of Contents

Acknowledgments   VII
Introduction   IX

One: A New View of You   1
Two   Perceiving Space   4
Three: The Internal Family Systems℠ (IFS) Model: A Universal Paradigm for Being Human   7
Four: Self-Inquiry: An Important Aspect of Mindfulness and Meditation   13
Five: Your Inner Dialogue: Who's Speaking? Who's Listening? Who's Leading?   17
Six: Gifts of True-Self Leadership: Journal Prompts and Self-Inquiry Practices   19
      1st Gift: Calm   22
      2nd Gift: Curiosity   24
      3rd Gift: Connectedness   27
      4th Gift: Clarity   31
      5th Gift: Compassion   34
      6th Gift: Confidence   37
      7th Gift: Courage   38
      8th Gift: Creativity   43
Seven: The Golden Rule Revised   47
Eight: Bringing True-Self Leadership into the World: Loving and Leading from the Inside Out   50
Nine: Instructions for the Self-Inquiry Tracking (SIT) Process   55

Afterword   60
The SIT Journal—30 Personal "Check-in" Pages   62

Acknowledgments

The ideas for this guide and self-inquiry process are based on the teachings of the Internal Family Systems℠ (IFS) Model— a universal paradigm for understanding human nature. I'd like to acknowledge my mentors and Senior Lead Trainers for the Center for Self-Leadership, Pamela K. Krause, M.S.W., L.C.S.W. and Chris Burris, L.P.C., L.M.F.T., who both believed in me and encouraged me to share my voice. I am so grateful for their healing support and have immense respect for their remarkable Self-Leadership. The essence of what I have learned from them is not only reflected in these pages, but also in my ever-expanding and joyful life.

I'd also like to acknowledge and thank Richard C. Schwartz, Ph.D., founder of the Center for Self-Leadership and the Internal Family Systems℠ (IFS) Model of Psychotherapy. His work has enhanced both my personal and professional life. He presents a clear and universal framework and practice which offers everyone a chance to live an empowered, compassionate, and meaningful life, learning to love and lead from the inside out.

Finally, to my family—Jeff, Kellie, AJ, and Holly—you have taught me the meaning of unconditional love. May you always know, believe in and rely on the awesome nature of your true Self.

INTRODUCTION

EVERY DAY, in my counseling office, I meet brilliant, successful, good-hearted people, young and old, who feel dissatisfied, unhappy, or confused about their life, their relationships, or their personal identity. Many people feel they are living a fake life. They feel like they are living to please others and are not being true to themselves. They want to experience some sort of change. They are wanting support, guidance, and clarity about who they are at their core, and about what needs to change in order to live more authentically. They want their outer life circumstances to change or they want to experience a different way of being. Either way, they want a more satisfying and meaningful life. I respect their effort to actively seek out what they are looking for, and I know they will find it within.

To one degree or another, we all long to *be* more or *have* more of something, like to be more relaxed, or have more freedom, more respect, or more love, enthusiasm, success, inner peace, or connection. You name it. Sometimes we can achieve what we want, but often our satisfaction is temporary. And, when we try to make changes and fail to feel fulfilled, we then become frustrated and confused. As these feelings set themselves deeper into our mind and heart, our longing and self-doubt begin to grow, and we become drained of our innate intelligence and power to create the life we desire. As we judge ourselves and everyone around us, we become our own worst enemy.

Are you searching? What is it that you want more (or less) of in your life? What's one thing you'd like to change about yourself? What are you willing to do to achieve it? What stands in your way? What choices need to be made in order for you to reach your highest potential, and find more happiness, or, at least some balance?

Many years ago, after a long, hard day of climbing, I laid down on the grass in the Grand Tetons region of Wyoming. As my body relaxed into the support of the earth, my eyes were pulled upward toward the massive, black sky. The thousands of stars, like points of light, took my breath away, beaming down on me, as if we were connected. As I tried to grasp their multitude and magnificence, it dawned on me that this is the abundance available to me. Each star a choice, an opportunity, a desire. I was shown in this night, all the many things I loved about life and all I wanted to experience.

This simple moment held profound importance to me. It offered me a deep sense of connection and a broader awareness of what it means to be alive. I experienced clarity about my creative power to desire and to choose, and I felt a deep gratitude that I had this privilege. I also felt a natural sense of compassion arise in that same moment, for those who may *not* have this freedom to choose about certain things. Somehow I felt connected to them also, and hoped that everyone would have someone who believed in their own potential. I decided that night, I wanted to be that believer and supporter for people.

My awareness felt transcendent that night, like I was in relationship with each and every star and each and every person. I felt outside the limits of my normal self, my normal thoughts, and concerns. I felt open to the regal

INTRODUCTION

presence and quiet confidence of the mountains, without a sense of ego, or separation. I was connected to them somehow, and to all of human kind. I experienced the stillness of that black night, like a heavy blanket, quieting my busy mind, dissolving thoughts of past and future. There was only the present moment and all it contained. With a palpable sense of calm and clarity about the harmony and well-being of everything, my awareness felt as open hearted as that sky, welcoming me into its joy. I realized this sense of pure awareness is rooted in the deepest part us. I knew, without a doubt, this state of being is who we really are underneath all the stress, worries, and planning which we hold dear, as part of our life, and our identity. After all, without a problem to solve, who would we be? If we can minimize all the turmoil of our constantly distracted mind, we can notice moments of greater clarity, compassion, and connection that make up the experience of deep living.

I hope you have had at least one experience like my night under the stars! And if so, I assume you want to have more, like I do. I think we all are wanting more of these precious moments of awareness, clarity, and peace. It's these moments that offer a different perspective on our day-to-day concerns, and give us a felt sense that there is something more, and that we are okay. They give us a glimpse of our profound connection to each other and to all that is, from a broader viewpoint. When in this state of being, there are fewer, (if any) beliefs or judgements obstructing our deepest knowing. We are clear about our power and desire to make choices for the benefit of all, and from this, we get a sense of the basic goodness of our true nature.

I have come to think of this type of awareness as seeing through the eyes of my true Self. Although the concept of the Self has been around for centuries in religious circles, you do not have to be religious or believe in God to live from a place of higher wisdom, authentic compassion, and deep connection. What if you were given a concrete, step-by-step method to manage internal obstacles (thoughts and feelings) so that you could better access this state of Presence in your daily life? Well, fortunately, I discovered this process many years ago, when I was introduced to IFS—which stands for Internal Family Systems℠. And, I am passing it along to you, today. It has changed my sense of Self and increased my capacity for Self-Leadership. As a result, I experience more feelings of calm, clarity, compassion, and confidence which ultimately have deepened and changed my ability to love, lead, and live with joy. Most of my clients who have learned this practice report the same result.

I warn you, this book has more questions than answers, because it's meant to be an invitation to explore your own inner world with contemplations and the daily SIT process. It is personal and experiential. I have taken the risk of being transparent about my own internal system and the transformation I have experienced in hopes of offering you more clarity about what's possible. My purpose is to encourage you to develop more trust, honesty, and love within yourself, thereby becoming more empowered to live, love and lead in the world. You will discover a universe within you, filled with deep desires and inner resources that may be stifled or hidden behind protective shields of limited beliefs, extreme emotions, or disturbing behaviors. These discoveries will be like trailheads which can guide you to go deeper, and lead you to a more joyful experience of life and relationships. No matter who you are, learning the steps of befriending yourself will help you in all that you do.

I wish you well and would love to hear from you about your experiences. Most of all, stay awake to the secrets of your inner world. There is beauty in the darkness.

CHAPTER ONE

A NEW VIEW OF YOU

One Christmas holiday, a dear friend gave me a beautiful gift. It was a small white porcelain figurine of a young woman, hair falling to her shoulders, and wearing a long flowing dress. She looked like she could have been an angel, but she had no wings. She was holding an infant in her out-reaching hands, showing the baby to a fawn, who was nose-to-nose with the baby. They both looked delighted to meet. There was such a feeling of tenderness and innocence in my heart as I looked at it. I was in awe for a moment. My attention became so absorbed in its world, that when my friend spoke, I was startled back to reality. She softly said to me, "She reminds me of you." I was *completely* shocked. "No way," I said. And, for months after that day, every time I looked at that figurine, I was puzzled... my friend's view of me was astoundingly different than my own.

We identify ourselves by what we perceive as our strengths and weaknesses, accomplishments and failures, talents, skills, religion, appearance, gender, (or non-gender), race, family heritage, and level of success, among other things. And, on another level, we define ourselves by what we think, feel, and do.

Sometimes our attitudes, emotions, and behavior stem from our cultural heritage, and we don't always understand why we feel or act the way we do. We seem to inherit attitudes and burdens as well as physical traits.

Additionally, we become who we are because of our experiences. We have developed morals and values and hold them as standards for what's right and wrong. Sometimes we take pride in our thoughts and behaviors, and sometimes we are embarrassed by them. We constantly create judgments about who we are as a person, and about the character of others. We identify with our thinking mind, and usually don't question our perspective. We are tied to our beliefs as if they anchored our existence. Unfortunately, mooring ourselves to our thoughts and beliefs limits our capacity to notice, understand, adapt, and direct our actions in wise and beneficial ways. Sometimes what we think are our strengths are actually weaknesses, and vice versa.

I invite you to notice all the different aspects of you, and the different moods that come and go on any given day. Do you like some, and despise others? Notice what really gets your blood boiling. How strongly do you believe certain things? When do your feelings get hurt? When do you close yourself off from others, and when do you join? We experience ourselves differently from week to week because our mind is multidimensional. Each part of us has various characteristics and motivations that have developed over time, and these parts of us influence us without our awareness.

There is an inner dialogue between these parts of us, which is happening constantly. Are you aware of that voice that criticizes you, or the part of you that is constantly trying to solve the next problem? Sometimes these parts of us are helpful resources, and sometimes they are not. With more consistent awareness of these inner voices, we can begin to realize that these parts of us are not who we really are. But this is possible only when we gain awareness and separate from them. We are actually much more than the sum of our parts, and this understanding can offer us a new sense of identity.

My friend could see and appreciate my deepest and truest Self as being tender and loving, because she had nothing interfering with her perception of me. I, on the other hand, could not see or relate to what she knew, because my internal voices of identity, judgement and perfectionism got in the way. Only when I became curious about my beliefs did I start to understand what I needed to do in order to soften their negative voices and clear the space they held in my mind.

CHAPTER TWO

PERCEIVING SPACE

I ONCE TOOK AN ART CLASS that taught me to draw things by looking beyond them. She showed us how to focus on and draw the space which held and defined the objects we saw. There was color and "life" in that space that I had never noticed before. As I drew what I "saw" in the space, the objects became the background and the space in between them became far more interesting and prominent. The picture had a fuller dimension. It felt more complete.

Years later, I went to a movement and dance retreat. There were about sixty of us packed in a small studio, nestled in the woods of the Hudson Valley. The world-famous NYC dance instructor, tall and willowy, floated around the room in her flowing handkerchief skirt, while she told us to form two concentric circles. As the percussionists began to beat out their exotic rhythms, the outer circle was instructed to move in a clockwise direction and the inner circle, counterclockwise, simultaneously. We were told to stay in rhythm with the fast pace of the drums as we moved around the room, interweaving with each other. It was total chaos! I wondered, "What in the world brought me here?"

We all bumped into each other, tripping and nudging, laughing and grumbling. It was a very annoying five minutes. She finally stopped the music, as if to pitifully acknowledge we had totally failed the task. The bewilderment in the room was palpable. Surprisingly, she expressed her understanding of how frustrating that little "exercise" was and praised us for hanging in there. Although her acknowledgement felt good, I still felt unsure and wondered, "what's next?"

Then, she told us to do the exact same thing, but *this* time move as part of the whole group, while looking for the space between the people coming toward us. The drums started again, and much to our surprise, we all moved forward with ease. There was now a sense of organization, clarity, and possibility. As we each looked for the space, we found it! We discovered that we could move toward each other in a harmonious way, without bumping into each other. The space in-between, which originally seemed sparse, became available to share. We were able to move as a group in a natural, flowing way. The contrast was shocking. There now seemed to be plenty of room to dance and move around. And we all felt like we were dancing together. By merely changing our focus, there was a new perception of unity, synchronicity, and leadership, as well as a sense of individual diversity, as each unique person related to one another in a shared experience.

I offer this story as a metaphor for the possibility of changing your focus away from all the thoughts and feelings that are dancing around in your head, taking up space, depleting your energy, and diverting you away from what's real. Instead, learn to cultivate space between the thoughts, and be aware of your life from that awareness.

The "space" I'm referring to, can be experienced when various parts of your mind stop judging, analyzing, planning, and ruminating. Sometimes this happens when you have an intense physical experience of something, and it draws your complete attention, like my night under the stars, or like the sensation of a long, lingering kiss, or watching the fiery colors of an August sunset, or watching the fairy-like magic of a dragonfly as it lands weightless on your knee. You become transfixed in a state of wonder. You lose your sense of time and space. You lose your sense of separate identity and become one with the object of your attention. Your awareness has qualities like soft, open, connected, and calm. A spacious, open mind allows these deep experiences, and is available to you when you gain the skills of Self-Leadership, which helps you navigate yourself out of the obstacle course of strong emotions and beliefs.

Meditation (paying attention) and setting intentions can take us into this open, quiet space, but we must first become still and listen to the inner dialogues which fill our mind, without pushing them away. Our mind can then become a friend, becoming still and open, allowing us to feel and focus on the present moment, without the chatter of our busy thoughts. As we hold our attention on whatever is noticed, we can moor ourselves to this anchor of Presence. This experience of your true Self can carry you beyond your individuality to the collective, holding for you your deepest love and highest purpose. Leadership from this space of awareness can offer unlimited possibilities for individual expression, love, and harmonious collaboration.

CHAPTER THREE

THE INTERNAL FAMILY SYSTEMS℠ (IFS) MODEL:
A Universal Paradigm for Being Human

I FIRST BECAME AWARE of the Internal Family Systems℠ (IFS) model of psychotherapy at a professional conference in 2011. It is now established as being one of the most impactful, evidence-based treatments in the field, for trauma and other mental health challenges. Additionally, it is now being taught in a variety of other settings, such as Universities, middle, and high schools, youth centers, community groups, mediation centers, corporations, churches, prisons, and sports organizations. This is because it offers everyone a healthy, useful understanding of how to maintain a sense of well-being and emotional balance, so we can navigate our life with more clarity, creativity, and joy.

Dr. Richard C. Schwartz, Ph.D., founder of the Center for Self-Leadership in Oak Park, Il. (www.selfleadership.org), developed the IFS model in the late 1980s while practicing family therapy in the Chicago area. He noticed that his clients with eating disorders spoke frequently about different "parts" of themselves which were in constant conflict. For instance, one part wanted to eat, and then overeat; another part hated being full and wanted to purge; and a third part was a harshly critical voice that then added a feeling of shame, which would start the cycle of binging all over again. At other times, the same clients described a sense of calm and clarity that arose when these other parts relaxed for a few days.

As Schwartz and his clients began to listen to these parts, it was clear that all parts were trying to help the client in some protective way. They all had good intentions, wanting to either numb intense feelings or prevent any sort of emotional pain from arising. He began to gather empirical evidence that the mind is multifaceted, having various parts of the brain which operate independently and powerfully to protect a person from perceived threat, even though that threat may be part of the past. These parts are attached to past experiences and act as though the situation is still the same in present time. They hold extreme thoughts, beliefs, and feelings, and usually obscure the presence of our true Self.

After working with dozens of clients who expressed the same experience, Schwartz found that his systems-oriented professional lens as a family therapist, worked as the perfect foundation for understanding that each of us has an internal family system of parts, represented by strong beliefs and emotions. These parts interact in similar ways as an external family, and it is the relationships between these inner parts that need to be understood and managed. In his most recent book, *Many Minds, One Self*, Schwartz builds a strong case, with much evidence, that the multiplicity of the mind is our natural state of being, not a pathological (Schizophrenic) condition. In fact, from the IFS lens, the condition of schizophrenia is adaptive, and held by a *part* of the person. It does not represent the whole person.

Like the facets of a diamond, these parts, reflect various aspects or sub-personalities within us, which serve us as inner resources when they are in balance. As these parts become more burdened, they begin to direct our lives from the perspective of their extreme beliefs and emotions. Our mind becomes filled with powerful feelings like distrust, anger, and jealousy. We end up losing sight of our Self as they take over our mind. We dissociate from being present, in varying degrees, because of fear.

Have you ever stayed in an argument long after you knew it was pointless? Or, said something horrible, just to hurt the person you love? How about a time when you became so nervous or anxious that your brain stopped working and you couldn't think? Or, when you have lost hours of sleep because you can't stop worrying? Or, you felt justified pouring your third glass of wine, even though you promised yourself you'd hold off tonight? These are examples of parts taking you over. And if you're not aware of what's happening, you lose your power to manage these parts of you. Your Self-Energy (your highest awareness and wisdom) is obscured and any chance for Self-Leadership is gone.

There are two types of protective parts that are held in our internal system. Schwartz has categorized them according to how they function. Their role is to protect a third category of parts known as our Exiles. These are the parts of us that we have shut away because they hold all the pain and memories of hurtful or traumatic experiences. Simply put, the internal system of protection is set up around the Exiles which not only hold painful memories, but also have feelings like inadequacy, worthlessness, and shame. The protectors are often afraid of their pain and vulnerability and do everything they can to protect the Exile from being activated. Schwartz teaches that certain Exiles carry such extreme emotions that they often become a governing force in our lives, determining our choices in relationships and driving us toward over-achievement, accumulation, and perfectionism. In other words, the extreme needs and desperation of these parts are so powerful, even from their exiled place in our system, they have a special unconscious influence over our decisions.

Managers protect in a proactive way, to prevent experiencing those painful feelings held by the exiles. They are strong and determined to do their job, and they have brilliant strategies for avoidance. As mentioned above, they push us to control our relationships and our environment so we won't get hurt. If we were to give descriptive names to some of these manager parts, we might recognize them as the Passive Pessimist, Inner Critic, Judge, Bum, Striver, Perfectionist, Dieter, Intellectual, or Know-It All. If we are not awake, they take over our mind and dictate our behavior, and we believe the parts are who we are. Not true! They're only a part of us.

Manager parts sometimes compete and polarize. For every part that pulls us in one direction, there is another part that eventually pulls us in the opposite direction. For example, saying, "I'm never going to do that again" after a bad experience may seem like a smart strategy, but it will lead to efforts to avoid and control things. We end up living a smaller life, avoiding risks, change, and opportunities for growth. And then, inevitably, we become unhappy again. Our unhappiness triggers another manager part who may believe we need to stand up and be heard, so it takes over, and pulls us into patterns of opposite behavior. It's like a tug-of-war.

Firefighters are a different type of protector than the Managers. They try to distract, soothe, calm, or numb us after painful emotions have been stirred up. These parts are reactive, rather than proactive in their protective function. For example, Firefighter parts drive us to use alcohol and drugs to numb or cool down the emotional "fire" of certain feelings. Or, we have a Foodie Firefighter which wants to reward, soothe, or nurture us when we feel exhausted, lonely, bored, or frustrated. These Firefighter parts give us reasons to work crazy hours, distracting us from stress at home, or perhaps to compensate for a sense of inadequacy.

THE INTERNAL FAMILY SYSTEMS (IFS) MODEL

Other types of Firefighters include those that cause self-harm, suicidal thoughts, dissociation, obsessions, and compulsions. Firefighter behaviors often cause significant problems; consequently, no one likes these parts. We then try to get rid of them with the preventative strategies of the Managers, previously mentioned. Managers always hate Firefighters, because they cause problems. Yet, they both are usually protecting the same Exile and don't know it. The answer lies in finding that internal space of your true Self to regain a higher perspective. This may only be possible by first taking some quiet time to compassionately listen with curiosity to all the parts that are working hard. Why are they afraid? What is their backstory? Their intention? If you listen deeply, you will hear and understand.

Most notably, the core concept of the IFS model is the true Self, which has the potential for healing and transforming the inner system, restoring its natural balance. It is the innate, eternal essence of who we are. It is our own individual Presence, pure awareness or consciousness or essential nature, which serves as our greatest resource, and offers wisdom beyond an entire lifetime of acquired knowledge. When we consciously differentiate from our parts, we can connect to our greatest source of clarity, wisdom, balance, and healing, but we must know how to access its energy.

Self-Energy is most available to us when our parts clear and we open space within. It is considered by some to be the life force that sustains us. It pervades everything, including us, as human beings. This energy is not only within us, but it expresses through us, as the intelligence of our best Self, as well as through our parts. When it is not restricted by extreme beliefs and emotions, this Energy can offer us a sense of aliveness, enthusiasm, intelligence, cheerfulness, and an intuitive sense of connection. We can actually feel sensation pulsating through our body, if we get still enough to notice it. Some people feel it as tingling or swirling, an overall relaxed state, or just the sensation of internal warmth; sometimes we notice a change in our voice. We might notice feeling deeply connected, calm, and caring, without an agenda to change things. There is always a relaxed broader awareness. As we learn to hold it and identify with it, we can use its wisdom and power to express more of our potential, because our parts have returned to their original resourceful state.

The IFS model describes Self-Energy as having eight essential qualities that we can experience: calm, curious, connectedness, clarity, compassion, confidence, courage, and creativity, all of which will be explored in more detail, later. I consider them the gifts of Self-Leadership because as we lead our inner world from the awareness of Self, they emerge and make living easier, and so much more fun. They rest in the natural innocence and trust of our Being. As we learn to unburden and transform our wounded parts, these natural qualities can infuse our daily experiences with purpose, meaning, success, vitality, and unselfish desire. It is the expression of these eight qualities, as the essence of our Self-Energy, that allows us to offer authentic Presence in our daily lives.

For those interested in learning more details about IFS, please go to www.selfleadership.org for a wide variety of books, DVDs and trainings, as well as a listing of therapists/practitioners world-wide.

CHAPTER FOUR

SELF INQUIRY:
An Important Aspect of Mindfulness and Meditation

I T IS IMPORTANT TO ESTABLISH a clear understanding of why the element of self-inquiry has been emphasized as the main focus of the SIT process, which differs from other, more typical meditation practices. Self-inquiry in this context, is a process of looking inward toward the thoughts, sensations, beliefs, emotions, and images you hold within your mind, heart, and body. As you are able to be curious, you can inquire about what's there and gain more self-awareness. With practice, we aim to notice our judgements and disdain about our Manager and Firefighter parts, and then inquire about those Critic parts, too. We want to try to be open and curious about every feeling and belief that arises. Eventually, we begin to develop a habit of self-inquiry as a momentary awareness that occurs periodically throughout each day. Becoming adept at noticing our thoughts, feelings, and bodily sensations as they arise, without judgment, is what I consider *mindful* self-awareness. Listening with curiosity is key.

Mindfulness relates to mental focus and is the ability to be aware of what is present, or what is happening in the moment, without judging it in any way. This focus applies to our inner world of thoughts and emotions, and also to the external world of circumstances. Mindfulness describes a state of mind during meditation, and/or daily life. Although a relatively new practice here in the West, especially in the field of psychology, it has been practiced in Eastern cultures for thousands of years. We apply the skill of mindfulness as we non-judgmentally notice the thoughts and feelings of parts as they arise in the present moment. With compassion and curiosity, we maintain our awareness and Presence, never rejecting or judging what we notice.

Meditation has a long history and many variations. It can be practiced for a few minutes, hours or even days at a time. Sometimes it is guided and other times it is done in complete silence. It can be done standing, sitting, walking, or lying down. The eyes can be open or closed. Often, in meditation instruction, you are guided to pay attention to your breath (single-minded focus) and you are asked to watch the thoughts that enter the mind, note (name) them without judgement, (mindfulness), and let them go (release). This is done to create an open, quiet mind. For some practitioners, this type of meditation process can facilitate a sense of peaceful awareness. For other people who may have busy thoughts, strong emotions, anxiety, or ruminating tendencies, meditation can be difficult to "master." Negative judgment may prevail, emotions may be loud, and distraction is incessant. In other words, our parts want more than to just be noticed and released! When the meditation time ends, some people feel refreshed and others walk away with a sense of frustration or failure, which then becomes an obstacle to future success.

I have had a long, on-and-off relationship with mindfulness and meditation. It began back in the mid-'70's, when, like other Eastern Baby-Boomers, I packed up my skis and escaped to the beauty and mystique of Colorado to "find myself," hike in the pine covered mountains, and go to graduate school. Conflicting desires, for sure. I met a guy who taught me to meditate. Since weed was not a good option for me, (though my Margarita-loving Firefighter was always on call), meditation offered a possible solution for my inner restlessness and racing mind.

At first I felt very cool, sitting on my cushion every morning, legs crossed (in the least painful way possible), trying to follow my breath, in and out, in and out. My analytical thoughts, creative ideas, worries, and plans would come and go, but frequently my tenaciously active mind would quiet down. I found some stillness within me while my thoughts were gently pushed to the side. But later, my ambitious and critical internal voices pushed back and took hold, reminding me I should quit meditating and work harder or I would never be good enough to get ahead.

In the '80's, the trend was to meditate by visualizing desired outcomes, and waterfalls washing away my fear and anger. I memorized hundreds of positive affirmations to over-ride my negative thoughts, still seeking a quiet happy mind. More often than not, I felt a heavy sense of hopelessness surround me like a dense fog. Even into the '90's, when yoga and meditation groups popped up everywhere, I found the slow pace unbearable. My mind just wouldn't shut up. "Just go run, or climb, or play tennis…you'll be fine," and I'd leave the class before savasana even began. Stillness was definitely not pleasant.

After that, came Thich Nhat Hahn, Jack Kornfield, Tai-Chi, and Shambhala practices. I learned the hard way, that my parts were *not* going to be denied. Please don't misunderstand—these masters and profound practices offered me many powerful and important gifts, but my internal parts needed *my* attention, and not to be "spiritually by-passed."

I know now, my negative view of myself was my greatest obstacle. There was nothing wrong with me, yet I was trying to improve, weed out, or push away my thoughts and feelings, because my inner critic was running the show. All that was needed was to listen to those thoughts, gain more understanding of their roots, open my heart, and embrace them. But, that is a frightening prospect when there are neglected Exiles waiting to be heard.

The past is very much alive in us, like a seed underground. It is carried by our inner children (or teens), stuck in the past. Even if you are not aware of its potential influence or how it impacts your present life, elements of your past are still driving you in various ways. When we add the combination of curiosity and self-inquiry to mindfulness and meditation, our awareness goes where it needs to be, and offers us the opportunity to connect with our neediest parts. Learning to care about the roots of what is present in our mind, heart, and body, and listen with kindness, rather than with disgust, can lead us down the very important path of a positive, trusting relationship within ourselves.

Our bodies hold our truth and all our stories. They need to be honored. If not by you, then by whom? When our inner most truths are heard and deeply understood, there is an integration of that part of you that has been exiled from your awareness. With a conscious and deliberate connection comes healing, and with healing comes space, and more stillness, and all the other gifts of Presence and Self-Energy. This is the transformative power of self-inquiry.

CHAPTER FIVE

YOUR INNER DIALOGUE:
Who's Speaking? Who's Listening? Who's Leading?

I F YOU HAVEN'T NOTICED, there is a constant inner dialogue going on in your head almost every minute of every day. On a good day, it might be a cooperative and collaborative one, or on a stressful day, it could be one of conflict and chaos. As we live from day-to-day, fulfilling responsibilities, managing our health, and engaging with others, our managerial parts believe it is their job to make all the decisions about how to be, what to do, and which version of us will show up. Choices about what to say during the meeting, what to wear, whether to go to the gym after work or go out with your co-workers, whether to tell your friend you know she's been lying, or, whether to accept the promotion, despite hating your job. It's somewhat "dangerous" to be oblivious to this dialogue!

If, for example, your inner "Defender" part is rehearsing how to tell off your interfering mother, and you aren't awake enough to speak for and lead this part, words will be said and decisions will be made from the angry part that cause damage to an important relationship. If you are aware of this part's need to set boundaries, you can speak on behalf of the part, and still convey the message without harm. This is Self-Leadership.

Often, the most powerful parts in our system are the Firefighters, who strongly step up and take over when something upsetting has happened, (or hasn't happened). We seem to be powerless over the strong urges and compulsions of these parts that want to save us, numb us, distract us, soothe us, take us away, or just yell at people. Although they have good intentions, they often cause behaviors that have negative consequences. Manager parts then arrive later, creating guilt, regret, self-loathing, and shame. If we don't maintain mindful awareness, then we aren't present, and we become dissociated (separated) from our Self. We need to pay attention, mindfully, and be curious about their intentions and fears, as they begin to drive us off the cliff with extreme behavior.

The theme of Self-love and leadership for this book, centers on the idea that it's time we take personal responsibility to manage, care for, and lead ourselves in a way that allows us to be a positive influence in our world (family, community, or workplace), rather than part of the problem. We can no longer afford to live unaware and unconscious. As we awaken to the truth about who we really are and what we are capable of being, we move toward our greatest potential, and a deeper, more meaningful experience of life. We can access greater power and wisdom that can brighten the world around us. When we are a Self-led person we see no use for controlling others, and there's no need for self-promotion, either. We naturally feel committed to service and have a spontaneous passion for life. There is no reliance on externally created moral or legal rules to make us do the right thing. We are naturally inspired with integrity and compassion to improve the human condition, because we know we are all connected.

CHAPTER SIX

GIFTS OF TRUE-SELF LEADERSHIP:

Journal Prompts and Self-Inquiry Practices

WHEN WE LEARN TO BE REALLY ALERT and mindfully self-aware enough to notice our emotions and strong beliefs as they arise, we can then listen, connect, and ask them to relax. We can take a pause, breathe in a few deep breaths, and then speak *for* that part of us, instead of from it. For example, I can talk to my co-worker, and describe my feelings and the impact of her sarcasm, instead of withdrawing with resentment or attacking with frustration. This is how we lead our parts with the caring presence of our true Self.

When we can create some mental and emotional space, we will notice many wonderful gifts emerge that help us, especially in relationships. When we are deeply present, without the need to control anything, the mind opens and they emerge. We do not have to manufacture an experience of them. They are natural qualities that already exist within us, beneath the surface. When available, these qualities help us "see" the deeper reality of things, help us understand others, and how the world works, as "unfair" as it might be. We can see the flaws in others and know that is just human nature. We are able to stop taking things so personally. We feel more connected, as our perspective broadens, and we realize that we all share the same human emotions of this life experience. It is worth the time it takes to cultivate and open up these qualities, each and every day.

A true story about the gifts of Self-Leadership: A few summers ago, I invited my cousin up to our cabin located in a very remote and isolated area in northern Quebec. The cabin is right on the lake, occupied only by loons and a few boaters with a line out, trolling for the big one. The place is surrounded by at least forty miles of forest on every side, and a lucky day is one in which we see a bald eagle fly overhead. There are no phones, electricity, or internet. I equate it to heaven, but it's certainly not for everyone. I'd been talking about it to her for many years, and she decided to join us that particular summer for five or six days. Of, course, as these things happen, it rained, no, poured, every day. It was cold and miserable. No hikes in the beautiful woods, no boating, or picnics on the beach in the warm sunshine. Only four people and two dogs stuck in a very small, isolated cabin. Everyone got cabin-fever by the fifth day, and the restlessness was building into lots of moody facial expressions, tense periods of silence, naps, and nibbles.

We each had parts that were trying to be nice, wanting to make the most of it. I had parts that wanted to have fun, trying to be creative about how to occupy our time, and other parts holding back frustration. I had a part that felt responsible for providing a good time as the hostess, another part that was anxious because I had a project that I wanted to work on, and also a guilty part that reminded me that my desires were selfishly rude. As time went on,

I felt more disconnected, as I withdrew deeper into my mind. Finally, all our repressed thoughts and feelings blurted out. I said something, and then she said something, and we were off—into the land of emotions and opinions!

As I stood there, feet firmly planted, defensively planning my next words, I suddenly woke up. It was like the lights went on, and I *saw* her. Really saw her *deeply*. I saw the pain in her tearful eyes. I heard the quiver in her voice. And, in a moment of pure awareness, I felt my heart soften—I sensed an expansion in my chest, and I felt a deep compassion for us both, as I remembered how much I loved this person standing in front of me. As my heart opened, so did hers, and as she noticed this shift she could then hear me and connect with me in a deeper, more open way.

I deliberately connected to my deepest Self and to my intention for peace, and told her, "I can see your pain and I don't want either one of us to suffer like this. I really love you and I don't want to fight." She agreed. It felt like someone else was talking through my mouth, yet I felt a strong internal strength and connection to myself and to her. I felt courage, and a humble type of confidence. I felt amazingly calm, and very clear that certain *parts* of us were at war with each other, despite our mutual love and friendship. She responded by saying that as she noticed a calmness come over me, her whole body relaxed, and she felt drawn into the space of love that I was offering. These are some of the physical effects that can be noticed when Self-Energy is flowing, and parts have receded to the background.

We then sat down and had a heart to heart conversation for over an hour about our various perspectives, speaking on behalf of our Manager parts and the Exiles they protect. We listened compassionately to each other and this deep witnessing was very healing. We both felt so much clarity and connection! It was a perfect mutual unfolding of the gifts of Self-Leadership, and we both felt a spontaneous unburdening.

These Self-Leadership qualities that we shared, include: calm, curiosity, connectedness, clarity, compassion, confidence, courage and creativity. In IFS, these are known as the eight Cs. An explanation of each is followed by some nature-based contemplation exercises, and also some Self-inquiry prompts which will direct your attention inward.

1ST GIFT: CALM

Calm is usually the quality we long for most often, especially in these stressful, busy times. For some of us, feeling calm is usually just a short and temporary experience. Sometimes we carve out time to be still and feel it, but not often enough. It usually feels like a luxury to feel calm, yet our greatest wisdom comes from listening to the stillness that's deep within. We may try taking a morning walk or getting out in nature, but we usually carry with us our busy mind and distracting cell phone. Why? Even when we try to get quiet, our mind rarely stops. Some of us try to meditate to quiet our mind, letting our thoughts go, but then we get off our cushion and life resumes its demands.

In daily life and especially in relationships, we all know how helpful it is to stay calm. Rather than lose ourselves to the emotions and rigidity of certain parts of us, if we know how to authentically relax in order to compassionately listen, think, and find some curiosity, we could be with the person in a deeper way. But, it's easier said than done!

What stands in the way of feeling calm? Why do parts of us always interrupt our attempts for peace with urgent reminders and concerns? Or, why do parts *fool* us into a false sense of calm by blocking our emotions to make us numb? Either way, they take up so much mental space and energy, trying to protect us, that there is no room for our natural sense of calm to arise. I have learned from listening to my parts that there are many reasons why stillness feels vulnerable. Some believe feeling calm and still just feels empty and uncertain. They want me to stay busy, analyzing, planning, and doing, so I won't waste time or be left behind. Another part believes that time is short and I must hurry to get it all done, or I will fail. Another part does not trust or want to feel my spacious Presence. Therefore, it distracts or annoys me.

What are your noisiest parts? What is their message or concern? Can you get still enough to listen? It is interesting to listen to the back story of the parts that interfere with your sense of calm. I have found listening to be the most successful strategy to quiet the mind. *Notice* your thoughts and emotions, but don't attach to them. Listen to the inner voice(s), but don't judge them. This habit of mindful Self-awareness is the beginning of reaching some inner stillness. Below is an example:

One morning, as I was doing my SIT process, I noticed some anger and frustration toward a loved-one as I tried to focus on my breath. I felt agitated and I couldn't relax or concentrate. I knew there was a part that had a lot to say! As I listened to that part of me, I learned that it felt I was being disrespected and treated in a demeaning way, in front of people I cared about. That small discovery helped me to immediately feel some compassion for it. I realized that the anger was an attempt by this part to set boundaries and be clear this was not ok. As I continued to sit and listen, I gradually felt calmer, and as I relaxed, my heart opened to this angry part of me…and I wrote these words from my experience:

> *"This calm feels like the stillness of the candle flame when it stops waving. It's the space between each breath, the sky between the clouds. Calm is still. Still is now. My body slows down. Calm is the natural field that holds my thoughts, like the darkness holds the stars. It's complete. The space—empty, yet full. Just awareness… that in this field, everything is connected."*

And, as you can tell, my anger completely melted away. I didn't have to reason it away, or work at forgiving the person, or ignore what I felt. By leaning into the anger, it was allowed to transform naturally. I was left with only a sense of deep compassion, connectedness, and love for me and for the person I once felt angry toward. With this sense of calm and understanding, I could then talk to the person, set boundaries, and speak for my anger instead of from it.

Enjoy your breath. Enjoy sitting in the spacious stillness. See the sky, instead of the clouds. Let go of all problems to be solved for a few minutes. What then remains? Stay in it, moment to moment, breath to breath, and allow your curious nature to unfold in the unknowing of this internal space.

Resourcing Nature for Calm:
Look at or think about the moon, shining softly against the black sky. Listen to its silence. Connect to its soft light. Breathe in its essence of calm. Notice it sits in the stillness of the dark empty night. That too, is calm, held in the stillness of space. This is the truth about you.

Self-Inquiry Practice for Calm:
Name the obstacles in your life that prevent you from feeling calm. What stops you from taking time to be still for fifteen minutes each day? Identify some thoughts and beliefs that resist the idea of sitting in silence—feeling peace and calm. Can you feel compassionate toward yourself? And, toward the parts of you that make you stay so busy and work so hard? Write about your insights.

2ND GIFT: CURIOSITY

The gift of curiosity offers us many things. It offers openness and desire to know something beyond what is already known. It maintains patience and genuine interest. It begins with a focused awareness in the present moment and moves us forward without an agenda. Life is much more interesting when we hold the gift of curiosity.

As we examine our inner world of beliefs and emotions, we aim to know more about their origin and function in our system. We are willing to give our time and attention to listen a little deeper, without judgment—like you would with a friend. As we do this for ourselves, we can also choose to do this with others. We set our intention toward being present and authentically curious, with an openness that feels safe and invites honesty. This kind of curiosity will bring connection and new possibilities for a better relationship within yourself and with others.

In our culture, there is a subtle resistance to being curious, because curiosity has to exist in a field of not knowing. And, not knowing something is not usually respected. It takes courage, or at least some humility to be open and honest like this. We normally create a sense of security by predicting, analyzing, and planning, based on what we know. And so, to be curious about someone, or a situation, or even about our own beliefs might feel risky. If we don't know, and don't pretend to know, does that mean we're stupid, uninformed, or naive? Will people think less of us? Maybe, unless they consider curiosity as valuable.

Another obstacle to curiosity is boredom. When, for example, we begin our SIT process, and notice that we're bored, or dreading the day ahead, we can be certain we have lost touch with our curiosity. Again, there's no openness to wonder what might happen. Our mind speeds along on auto-pilot, "knowing" and making predictions of what will occur, based on the past. We often expect to experience the same things over and over, and even if they were to happen differently, we would experience them in the same way, because we are not present. We are not noticing in the moment what's actually in front of us. Our parts are on automatic. We are disinterested. A curious mind would ask questions like, "I wonder what this will be like?" or, "I wonder what he really thinks?" or, "Is there a part of me that is blocking my curiosity, and if so, why?"

Curiosity requires a "beginner's mind," a mind that is more spacious than full. We are aware that knowledge, education, and expertise are important and valued in our American society. But, as we educate ourselves, and become more knowledgeable, we need to guard against becoming closed and too full of what we know. Certain attitudes can limit our openness for new awareness.

This reminds me of the well-known tale of an educated professor who went to a Zen master to become knowledgeable about Zen. As they sat down to talk, the Zen master poured them some tea. He filled the professor's cup, and then kept pouring the tea until it over flowed onto the table. As the professor demanded for him to stop, the teacher replied, "Your mind is like this cup: It is too full of your own knowledge and opinions to receive any more! How can you learn anything new without emptying your mind first?"

Uncertainty can feel insecure. When we believe we need to be the one who is right, we become cut off, separate, and competitive with the world. Without confidence, we equate curiosity with not knowing—with ignorance. Without curiosity, we lose perspective and stay stuck in old ways, as everything else around us changes. Conversely, as we become more open, curious, and compassionate with ourselves, we can then become more interested in others. We can naturally meet them with Presence, and offer them a space to be totally authentic, as their true Self. This type of interaction is mutually satisfying and trustworthy. Curiosity can open new doors of connection and clarity if we follow the path of our interests and awareness. Many wonderful things can be discovered.

At a poignant point in my IFS training, I heard a line from one of Rumi's poems that intrigued me, *"...The breeze at dawn has secrets to tell you, don't go back to sleep. You must ask for what you really want—don't go back to sleep..."* I felt like I was sleeping though parts of my life until I awakened and consciously became more curious. Life is now much more interesting and meaningful. I feel more involved and open to new possibilities.

Resourcing Nature for Curiosity:
Watch a sunrise or sunset. Or go to YouTube and look for "Relaxation Sunset Meditation in Hawaii." It's beautiful. Watch the sky and the waves. Notice your mind. Are there parts of you that get restless and bored? Notice whether you can relax and breathe slowly, through the whole thing, being curious about what will happen next. Things change, moment to moment. Can you wait with an open mind and heart?

Self-Inquiry Practice for Curiosity:
Are you rigidly attached to a certain opinion or point of view? If so, what is it? Where did you acquire this view? How does this view impact your life? Your relationships? Do you notice a feeling of defensiveness or resistance to these questions? Can you be curious about all of this?

3RD GIFT: CONNECTEDNESS

With a calm and curious mind, we can feel open. And, with this openness, our sense of connection can be felt internally. When we are aware and fully present, we can sense non-verbal signals and information coming toward us from others, beyond what they are saying. If we feel a type of resonance with that person, it can be translated into a sense of connectedness. We feel in harmony with that person, and trust begins to develop. That same harmony and trust can also be developed among various parts of us, in our own our internal system, if we focus on this intention. In the outer world, we feel this connection when we intuitively feel seen, heard, or understood. When we listen to our parts, they also feel seen and understood, and that is when a trusting relationship begins within. As this internal trust and connection build, a sense of authentic security and confidence develop. Our instinctual needs for safety and belonging are met, without seeking these things from someone else.

Ideally, we develop this sense of safety and connection from our early caregivers. When the adults in a child's life offer their full Presence and attention in loving ways, this attachment can provide the child a sense of security, identity, and confidence in the world. Unfortunately, we do not always have a secure attachment in early childhood, and this disturbed early connection can create limiting beliefs and strong emotions as protective parts become stronger, and inhibit our ability to love, trust, and connect to others, as adults.

It takes courage to let go of the caution we might hold when faced with the chance of getting close to others. It can feel risky and difficult to trust love or friendship. Independence might feel safer—more reliable. We may have parts that are friendly and accommodating, but they keep the relationship superficial, never depending on anyone, emotionally, in fear they will let us down. These parts, which are wounded and holding pain need your Presence and compassion, in order to unburden their old beliefs and heal.

One morning, as I did my SIT, I contemplated this idea of connectedness in relation to some friendships that felt empty to me. When I listened with curiosity, a sadness was revealed. A memory emerged about a time when I was around thirteen, and felt more connected to my sense of spirituality (God) than I did to people. I remembered one Sunday, sitting alone in church, on the burgundy velvet cushion, in the smelly old wooden pew, with my head buried in the hymnal, looking for the page of the next hymn. As I stood up to sing the words about love, I felt exposed and vulnerable, because I knew I was about to cry. I felt so empty and alone, among all these people. Why? Unfortunately for me at the time, singing always opened my heart, and so the tears began to flow, and continued flowing beyond my control. Holding back as much as possible, my embarrassment grew, knowing my cover had been blown, and my invisible pain was now visible. The hymn seemed to last forever as I tried to regain my composure.

As the hymn ended, I gathered up enough courage to sneak a peek around to see if anyone saw me, and I realized that no one had noticed me *at all*. Not one single "Good Samaritan" in that huge church was aware of my suffering. (A part of me *didn't* want to be noticed, but another part wanted some connection.) No fellow church member, family friend, neighbor, or stranger in the surrounding pews had noticed. Or, if they did, no one let on. I remembered feeling really shocked and even more isolated. This is why my heart feels empty now, I thought. No one was there back then, to offer comfort, or a warm glance or a soft hand on my shoulder to say, "I see you, and I'm sorry you're so sad."

It was the same every Sunday for six years, until I finally left my hometown. The good news is, one Sunday, while I was sitting in the same smelly pew, I literally saw the image of what looked like the face of Jesus, blended into a gold, gilded mosaic design, painted on the ceiling above the altar, and he seemed to be looking directly at me. My stomach flipped, and I was caught in shock and disbelief. As I paused and continued to stare, a sense of deep peace, connection, and energy washed over me. My mind slowed down, everything seemed quiet, and as I walked out of that powerful experience and carried on with my life, I felt seen and heard and comforted, beyond anything I can explain. Maybe a part of me created this illusion, and you have a part that thinks I'm a crazy "Holy Roller," but whatever it was, I experienced it in my body, not just my mind. It made me feel content and whole. Everything was suddenly alright, like the time I was under those Wyoming stars...

I always returned to that beautiful church, whenever I needed a sense of connectedness, not necessarily with people, but within my own heart. I now have a sense of deep love for those people, many of which are my friends, but this example serves to demonstrate how the simplest of experiences can have a big impact, due to the interpretation of our parts, who carry extreme beliefs and emotions.

Many parts of me developed strong beliefs during those early years, and my heart began to close. One protective belief that a part of me developed was, "If I stopped needing people, I couldn't be disappointed or hurt." I then became emotionally independent and extremely self-reliant, unwilling to trust or love with an open heart. And, because of this unconscious decision (made by a part of me), I was unable to sense a connectedness in a way that allowed confidence or compassion, beyond the superficial. More layers of protection grew, which held anger, resentment, and judgment. These layered over the hurt and disappointment, until dissatisfaction and separation prevailed in all my relationships throughout my twenties.

I had *little* awareness of my underlying hurt, (my exiled part)—only a sense of distrust, loneliness, and blame. I stayed busy as a perfectionistic high achiever, and developed a false sense of confidence. In fact, it wasn't until I worked with an IFS therapist that I was able to look deep inside me with compassion instead of criticism, and eventually unburden these extreme beliefs, and heal the wounded Exile. There is now more space in me for my true Self to be authentically present. My relationships are open hearted, safe, and loving. This is the power of Self-connection, compassion, and internal leadership, which allow the flow of Self-Energy to heal us with love from the inside out.

In the stillness of our own being, we can access a sense of connection, as we direct our attention to the parts of us that we have exiled, bringing compassion and hope. This develops trust and brings unity, strength, and confidence to our internal family, and allows us to then connect to others in a deeper way. With the idea of unity, we can open channels of kindness and acceptance, merely as part of our true nature, knowing we all share feelings of loneliness, inadequacy, and self-doubt. We can feel partnership rather than competition, trust rather than suspicion, forgiveness rather than resentment, equality rather than bigotry, similarity rather than difference.

Resourcing Nature for Connectedness:
Go to the woods or a local park where there are trees. If this is impossible, find a picture on the internet of the woods or forest. Sit, or imagine sitting among the trees, as if you belonged. Breathe in the air and smell the earth. Imagine the tree roots beneath you, intertwined with one another. A whole network of roots harmoniously connecting to one another, providing stability to the earth—and a secure foundation for you, on which you can rest. You too are connected, within yourself to all parts of you. As you offer your attention to your internal world with kindness and gratitude, you provide stability for your system. As you realize your energetic connection to the Self of others, you become part of the network of stability for your world. What do you notice when you think about this?

Self-Inquiry Practice for Connectedness:
What parts of you do you try to hide? For example, your anxious part, your inner critic or perhaps the part of you that makes you overeat or overwork? With an open mind, could you connect with one of these parts, that you may not like? Get to know it like a new friend? Ask this part why it acts/feels this way? What does it want for you? What's its job in your system? What is it afraid would happen if it didn't do what it does? As you listen, can you find some compassion in your heart for these parts of you?

4TH GIFT: CLARITY

In this context, the clarity I am speaking of is one of direct, objective awareness. It is unobstructed knowing—feeling like a laser-beam of certainty and insight, arising from a deeper, higher wisdom that transcends our everyday knowledge. It's important to keep in mind that awareness is different than thought. Awareness is noticing what is actually there, without opinions or interpretation. Thoughts are subjective and limited mental constructs that are generated from the mind in order to make meaning, in relation to what we already know. As we think, we automatically manipulate new information to fit it into our personal lens of perception.

Awareness, on the other hand is more objective and immediate. You are merely observing, through the five senses what you notice, in the present moment. If your awareness comes from being deeply present, your true Self will see and understand in a broader way than the limited views of your parts. Remember, parts hold extreme beliefs and emotions, and are always preoccupied by either the past or future. They hold various perspectives, based on experiences. From those experiences arise generalizations, fears, and conclusions which crowd the mind with worries, strategies, and advice. There is little space for the clarity that can arise when the parts give space for you to really be there, in the moment.

You may discover, as you begin your SIT process, that there is more confusion than clarity, depending on how much noise there is in your mind. In fact, you may get annoyed at your inability to watch or identify thoughts because they are moving so fast. Left unattended, this kind of "monkey mind" will cause stress, agitation, poor judgment, and indecision. This is the perfect time to stay in your seat, open your heart, and listen. Wait. Breathe. Clearly there is something important going on inside that you need to understand and attend to. Do not fear the mental chaos.

When clarity is missing, life is much harder. Sometimes it feels like a curtain closes or a wall goes up and a heavy veil of confusion covers over you. Everything becomes a chore. The mental activity creates uncertainty and self-doubt, yet we pretend we are fine, and carry on. Then anger slips out and we say something we regret, pushing people away in attempt to hide our overwhelm.

In contrast, pure awareness brings clarity, because it lacks normal thoughts of judgement. It feels spacious and open, and can only exist when our thoughts (parts) quiet down. It arises from the quiet stillness of our inner being. Patience is key, as we find balance between listening to those voices and negotiating our way to a calmer state. It's worth the time and effort to stay present, sitting until it emerges. Your clarity is definitely there, buried underneath the confusion.

As you breathe mindfully and ask for space from cluttered thoughts, something opens up. You begin to feel embodied, grounded, and present. You regain a sense of Self. Holding this Presence, you can ask your parts what they need from you today. You will then gain enough clarity to understand what emotions are present, and what you need to do to gain relief. During the day, as you hold your present-moment awareness, you will have access to your intuition and higher wisdom.

Resourcing Nature for Clarity:
Imagine looking up at a cloudy sky, filled with different shades of gray, all swirling and moving in no particular pattern. The clouds vary in their density and height. They break apart and then blend together. You sense a storm coming but don't know from which direction. You sit and watch. Then you notice the wind die down. The clouds slow their movement and begin to break apart. Slivers of blue sky begin to separate the clouds until their formation becomes clear. You can see each cloud's unique, individual shape, and you focus on one at a time, as the sky expands and opens. There is a sense of spaciousness. Soon, the sunlight is radiating throughout blue sky, and your view is bright and clear. The clouds are your thoughts and feelings, held in the realm of your open awareness. They come and go in your Presence, but you are their dwelling place, permanent and welcoming.

Self-Inquiry Practice for Clarity:
In what area of your life do you lack clarity? Is there something, some decision you are conflicted about? Notice if you can identify two polarized parts of you with differing perspectives on a subject. Can you listen objectively with curiosity to both sides? What are the fears of each side? What does each side hope to gain as an outcome?

5TH GIFT: COMPASSION

Compassion centers on awareness and could be considered to be an emotional state of caring for others. We feel sad for them when they suffer, and have a desire to eliminate their pain. When we feel compassionate toward a friend who is hurt, we feel concern for them and want to help. We understand, and perhaps remember a time when we suffered, and we are able to put ourselves in their experience. When we are open to receive compassion from a friend, it brings a sense of mutual connectedness. We feel cared for, comforted, and supported. We are more likely to share with them the details of our painful experience and what it was like for us. As they listen, we feel witnessed, understood, and cared for. We know we're not alone. The experience of compassion is healing and transformative. This is exactly how it works in our internal world as we attend to the needs and suffering of our parts. When we are compassionate with ourselves, we can learn to embrace our imperfections and build "shame resilience," to use one of Brené Brown's terms. This is what we want to develop for each part of us.

The problem is, we are often our own worst enemy. When we have critical or untrusting parts of us that block our compassion for others, we deny ourselves this sense of connection. Our critical parts also stop us from being compassionate with ourselves, making healing from past hurts impossible. The inner voice of our critical parts tell us things like, "You don't deserve sympathy, love, or compassion." Or, "It is your own fault." Or, "You'll never be good enough." Or, "You'll never win." There is old pain and shame that hide underneath those negative beliefs, and they will prevent the power of compassion to bring healing to yourself and to others.

Richard Schwartz, founder of IFS and the Center for Self-Leadership talks about the compassion that comes from our true Self as being much deeper than that which comes from one of our parts. It's more than just the comforting phrases we offer ourselves when stressed. He believes that genuine self-compassion is a journey into the multiple parts of ourselves—the good, the bad, the ugly, the confused—the frightened, the abandoned—so we can make friends with those parts on the deepest level. The primary obstacle to treating ourselves more kindly is the fact that most of us are addicted to self-criticism. As he points out, who among us hasn't had the experience of learning to be judgmental of ourselves as a teenager, when we're so worried about how we're going to appear to others? ...And, many times this self-criticism can easily turn into self-hatred.

The good news is, current researchers like Kristin Neff, Ph.D., show us that self-compassion is possible for everyone to learn and practice, no matter how critical, spiteful, and disconnected the person has been. From an IFS perspective, this is because compassion is an innate quality of our true essential nature, only needing to be reclaimed and perhaps practiced after years of being obstructed by harsh self-criticism. We can gain access to this natural tendency as we ask our cynical and critical parts to soften, giving our true Self a chance to be present. As we begin to transform our pain and shame, and regain our perception of our innate worthiness, we can see the world and ourselves a little differently. We actually empower ourselves to heal as we begin to understand the depth of suffering we have lived with, at the hand of our own inner critic.

Resourcing Nature for Compassion:
Imagine a flower in early spring, sprouting up from the dark, warm earth, petals tightly wrapped together to protect itself from the harsh chill of the morning air. As the sun rises and offers its light, the flower opens to the nurturing warmth of the sun's presence. The warm sunlight invokes the flower to rise and grow, offering it the perfect conditions in which it can open and blossom with the beauty inherent to its true nature... Imagine there is a supreme, divine, benevolent light offering you love and compassion. Feel the warmth of this light all around you now. Imagine breathing in this light—bring it into your mind and heart. Breathe it into each dark corner where pain may be hiding. Let this light bring in compassion and healing for all parts of you. See this light radiating from you, surrounding and permeating those you love, those in your community, and encircling the Earth. Know that you can open to this light of compassion any time.

Self-Inquiry Practice for Compassion:
What does your self-critical part say to you? What thoughts, emotions, beliefs and actions do you like least about yourself? Try to listen to these parts of you, asking yourself:

- *How do I feel toward this part of me?*
- *No matter what, can I open up some curiosity about it?*
- *What is the story behind it?*
- *What does it want? Why?*
- *What would happen if I didn't feel, think, or act this way?*
- *Am I willing to befriend this part with some self-compassionate understanding?*
- *If not, what is the story behind the internal resistance? What's the "downside" of being compassionate?*

6TH GIFT: CONFIDENCE

Confidence comes from a clarity of who we really are and arises as a natural quality of our true Self. It is a knowing, a remembering of our resiliency to bounce back from life's setbacks. When we fail at something meaningful, confidence offers assurance that we can get up and start again, because the strength is there. We will somehow figure it out. It's a belief in the power of our authentic Presence, and maybe even a faith in the best of our resourceful parts to step in and do what they do in order to help us keep moving forward.

No doubt, life has a way of diminishing our confidence. As children we experience times of hurt, rejection, embarrassment, and failure. Depending on the reactions of others, we can develop beliefs about ourselves which block our innate sense of capability. For example, if we become a perfectionist, to compensate for past criticism and failure, we soon discover it is a set-up for a continued sense of inadequacy. And, as self-doubt develops and takes over, it immobilizes us. We then consistently hesitate to try new things, speak up, or take action. This fear leads to decisions which create the very things we are trying to avoid: a sense of unworthiness and unrelenting self-doubt.

Things can begin to change as we bring self-compassion to the fear, defensiveness, and pain held within us. As we lean into our fears, instead of accommodating them, we can learn why we feel the need to be cautious. As we offer our true Presence and kind attention to our stories of failure, humiliation, and rejection, these experiences don't need to overwhelm us. As we take a step back and remember our true, essential nature, our natural confidence arises, and we can open ourselves to new possibilities, as long as we know we can rely on ourselves to support rather than be critical of our internal world.

Confidence is not just about believing in your Self, but it also is feeling like you're good enough to be around other people, that you have something unique to offer. You feel worthy of respect, friendship, and the goodness that is felt through open-hearted connection. You are comfortable in your own skin, and people sense it. People respond positively and you become a leader without trying to be, because you are genuinely open and authentic. You feel inspired and safe to share what's in your mind and heart, without too much concern for the reactions of others, because you hold unconditional love and respect for yourself. Your relationship with all aspects of you is solid. You truly want the best for all.

Resourcing Nature for Confidence:
Envision the Pacific Ocean's huge, powerful waves moving out, onto the shore. These waves build their dimension and momentum from the energy of their source, always connected to it and returning to it. The waves have no agenda to create change, yet they do. There is an internal, natural power and strength within them. They spontaneously respond to the conditions that surround them. Experience yourself as a wave, moving through your days with certainty, direction, and strength, balanced in your constant return to your Source for the next inspiration.

Self-Inquiry Practice for Confidence:
When do you feel most confident? Under what circumstances do you most easily believe in yourself? What or who causes you to doubt yourself? Why?

7TH GIFT: COURAGE

We experience the gift of courage when we do not let our thoughts and emotions stop us from doing something we need to do. Instead, we follow our inner knowing regarding what needs to happen and we take action in the midst of danger or risk. Sometimes the impulse of "yes" is just merely there, in our consciousness, pulling us toward a positive outcome, like in the case of someone needing to be rescued.

Acting with courage does not necessarily mean there is no fear. Fear is often sitting side-by-side with our courage, as we move forward. If we are curious about our fears and doubts, we will find that they usually have something to do with the outcome, and we can't always predict what that will be. Fear of the unknown can be a big obstacle.

Fear in our inner world of parts develops after being hurt, abandoned, rejected, or criticized. Or, after seeing someone we love be hurt in some way. With these experiences, we conclude we are unlovable, or never good enough, powerless to change anything, or worthless without the approval of others. We guard against being hurt again, by becoming really good at pleasing others, sensing what they want, and how to fit in. We never take a stand on tough issues, or step out of our comfort zone. Our courage to be authentic is masked by our need to stay emotionally safe.

On the contrary, overriding our fears without listening to them, by *trying* to be brave can potentially lead us toward destructive and harmful outcomes. Bravery, when coming from a fearful part creates distrust in our system because it is not authentic. Taking action when there is no discernment or inner alignment is an attempt to stand firm in a forceful and defensive way, without any foundation, wisdom, or strength. Others will sense this artificial courage and move on with disrespect.

With true Self-awareness, we can notice our impulses to act in defensive ways and learn to bring compassion to our fears, listening to those protectors with curiosity. As we do, we will realize the pain and negative beliefs we hold about ourselves as being the underlying cause of our fear. As we continue to offer compassion and connection to these deeper places in us, the fear relaxes and there is more space for courage to arise naturally. Authentic fearlessness is the result of new perspectives gained as transformation of fearful beliefs occurs. This type of courage arises from the true Self. We then gain awareness that we are more than what we normally acknowledge. We discover that there is incredible strength, just beneath our conscious awareness—a rope we can grab and ascend, bringing us to a higher viewpoint than the grip of self-doubt, fear, and powerlessness. We learn through experience that our true nature yields confidence and faith.

Believing in the innate goodness of our truest and most basic nature—our Self-Energy—is at the core of authentic human bravery. As we face the great problems in the world, no doubt, fear will be part of the experience. Therefore, we must stay awake and aware of our own inner battles and bias. Only when we are mindfully aware of fear as it arises, can it relax in the presence of our loving attention.

Below are some notes I wrote one morning about fear and courage, as I worked through the steps of the SIT process:

Step 1: Center: *I tried to focus on my breathing, my mind was scattered and busy. Breathing was shallow.*

Step 2 Notice:
a). *I noticed my Thoughts/Feelings/Bodily Sensations: shy, meek, queasy, small, unimportant, invisible, unmotivated, tired, unable to accomplish anything—I just want to stay home.*
b). *I noticed that I was feeling authentically curious and compassionate…I feel badly that I have parts that are feeling this way. There seemed to be some sadness, too. I wondered why.*

Step 3: Listen: *As I sat quietly, asking why, I realized there's a part of me that is afraid of failing today, if I dare try to help anyone or speak up or attempt anything,*

I'll mess it up... I feel chaotic, swirling nervous sensation at the center of my body... As I stayed with it, and kept focused on it, a memory arose: A very young part of me remembers feeling scared and powerless as a child, in the midst of endless conflict. Scared of the noise and the unknown, but wanting to speak up and say, "Stop! What's wrong? What's happening?" As I remembered these feelings, I felt compassion arise, my heart opened, and I just sat quietly. I felt I was really there with this young inner child. I realized how brave she (I) was... I actually experienced the courage it took to hold her ground in the midst of that chaos—staying present and centered when she was afraid and wanted to speak up or disappear. Despite her thoughts of fear and worry, she carried on with her daily life, but was always on guard. Despite all this conflict, which was out of her control, she somehow knew that it would all turn out okay... She knew that things would be better in the morning... I remembered my grandmother's words, "This too, shall pass." Her resiliency and courage created faith in herself. She knew there was some sort of inexplicable strength, beyond hers, and she was connected to it. Something unseen but powerful and supportive... As I continued to experience these memories, my body relaxed and I felt proud of that young child and told her so in my mind. And then, the images all faded away, and I was left with the awareness of why I felt so afraid and inadequate this morning...

The previous night I had watched a lengthy news report on the nationalists' rally, "Unite the Right," in Charlottesville, Virginia, protesting the removal of Confederate statues. Horrible scenes of hatred, bigotry, and racial violence went on and on for several minutes. I couldn't believe what I was seeing. Going to bed with these images impacted my mind with old feelings of fear, confusion, and a sense of powerlessness. Without conscious awareness, the TV news had awakened old hurts, and I was carrying these feelings into the next day. If I had not taken the time to sit with myself and curiously listen, these fears would have interfered with my day. I didn't push away my self-doubt, but faced the old stories with compassion instead of judgement.

After this process, I felt stronger, with more understanding, self-respect, and appreciation. No longer would the self-doubting part of me need to minimize my day...

Step 4: Negotiate/Ask: *I sensed a trusting connection within me, and felt an authentic desire to feel my courage and confidence! I wanted to focus and remember these True-Self qualities throughout the day, as being part of my essential nature. So, I asked within, if this self-doubting part felt my understanding and presence—I asked my fear and self-doubt to relax. I asked for space, so I could be fully present as I went through my day.*

Step 5: Open/Own It: *As I then began to relax and notice my breathing again, I let these ideas wash over me, I felt more spacious inside, more focused—lighter...my mind was quiet...it occurred to me that courage is the absence of obstacles. It moves us, and allows us to take action. It enables us to hold our most powerful Presence without doubt. Courage is the product of an inner knowing of our connection to all that is—to the confidence of knowing who I am... and that there is something to rely on, that always has my back. Then I felt other Self-Energy gifts arise, like connection, confidence, and clarity. It felt like these qualities spontaneously unfold—one from the other without any effort on my part...*

Step 6: Remember and Reinforce: *I made a note of my intention to remember "Courage" today, and put the word "Courage" on my phone calendar. I then set an appointment with myself to take a break in the afternoon to just get quiet and listen to whatever was happening inside me.*

Hopefully, this example of using the SIT process demonstrates how a few minutes of curiosity, self-awareness, and compassion can allow us to lead our day with more strength and authentic presence, not being hijacked by defensive parts and old pain that sometimes layer onto present-day situations. We do not do this process to become passive, but instead, to become clear about what action to take from the discernment of our highest perspective. Looking within, toward the discomfort we normally try to avoid, helps us build the courage we need to act.

Resourcing Nature for Courage:
Think of a tall mountain. See its broad base, connected to the Earth. It is an extension of its source, built up by the rising push of the Earth's tectonic plates. Its form is shaped by winds, rain, snow, and ice, but its presence remains strong and steady, despite the weather that comes and goes. Feel yourself grounded like the mountain, unshaken by the ever-changing "weather" of moods and circumstances that come and go.

Self-Inquiry Practice for Courage:
What are some of your deepest fears? When and why did they arise? Can you find the courage to explore them, offer compassion, and befriend these parts of you that hold fear? There's nothing that takes more courage than to look honestly within yourself.

8TH GIFT: CREATIVITY

Creativity is a personal experience, different for each one of us—hard to define and impossible to predict. Yet, when we are gifted with times of creativity, it's fun and exciting. We may feel more alert, awake, and alive. The flow of ideas feels fresh and new. Sometimes it feels like inspiration from a deeper place, from a source of intelligence beyond us. I have noticed that when new ideas arise, they seem to carry a strong desire to express. They don't feel the same as other intellectual ideas that come from thinking parts. This type of deeper inspiration comes from the higher intelligence of our true Self.

My most creative times are when my mind is calm, open, and focused in the present moment, like when I'm feeling the hot water in the shower or smelling a forest full of Balsam pines. My mind is focused on only what is happening now—no past or future, no beliefs, no extreme emotion, except maybe joy. This kind of focus quiets the mind and allows space for the creativity, and other Self-Energy qualities to emerge. As we do our SIT process, we can deliberately quiet and open our mind, as we ask our parts to relax, and open space for new, creative ideas.

Elizabeth Gilbert speaks of creativity or inspired ideas as having a life-energy all their own. She believes they have an impulse to manifest, and they need a partnership with a creator to become realized. That the *source* of creativity may not always originate from the human brain, but may come from some other source of unmanifested universal energy which we can access as our own. This creative energy offers inspiration, and if we say yes to it, it's ours to deliver. If there's no place for this idea or energy to "land" in us, because of self-doubt, unawareness, or fear, then it "moves on," according to Gilbert.

In terms of IFS and Self-Leadership, I offer you this: No matter how you define creativity, it is part of your divine nature and every other quality of your true Self will help you access and build your innate creative potential:

- *Calm* mind allows the still, quietude to hear new ideas as they approach.
- *Curiosity* opens you into the spaciousness needed for new possibilities to land.
- *Connectedness* provides the link, inside and out, to have access to new ideas and everything else you need to create and finish what you start.
- *Clarity* brings a certainty of higher purpose, a vision of what's good for all concerned, and a discernment and recognition of the parts of you which interfere with your creative Self-Energy.

- *Compassion* offers warm hearted kindness towards others who doubt you, and to the parts of you that are doubtful, fearful, managerial, and protective.
- *Confidence* reminds you of who you really are and what's important—namely that you are capable and worthy of living creatively and spontaneously, rather than predictably, needing approval, or a certain outcome to occur.
- *Courage* allows fear to come along on your creative journey, enabling your creative process to continue rather than end because of self-doubt or negative predictions of the outcome.

It is certain that the world needs your Presence, and your divinely inspired creativity. And we need creative, compassionate ways to bring out the best in others! In such a competitive world, we need inspired, creative solutions to the social and institutional problems that have existed for many decades and are now being exposed. We all know we can't solve problems at the level at which they occur. We need to get above the power struggles in a Self-led way. Developing trusting relationships, internally and in the outside world, will allow us to encourage each other in ways that will benefit us all. Creativity can bring new life to imbalance and old stagnation. It's time we step up, access our courage, and stop living small.

Resourcing Nature for Creativity:
Anything and everything in nature can teach about the miracle of its boundless creativity! Walk along a riverbed, stream, ocean, or lake. Stop and notice how the water at its edges has shaped its earthly borders, how the pebbles, rocks, or grains of sand are created by the interaction of the water. Or, stop and notice a flower. Buy one if you have to. Look deeply into its blossom to see the intricacies of its complex

color and beauty. Know that this creative energy is part of your own true nature. You only need to access it.

Self-Inquiry Practice for Creativity:
List some creative projects on your bucket list. Or, bring to mind a social problem you would like to help resolve. Try to open your heart, noticing any emotions that arise. What stops you from proceeding with your desire? If you don't have anything you want to do, sit in silence, focused on your soft, smooth breathing. Empty your mind. Imagine sitting in a dark velvet-like cave. Allow calm to emerge and be aware of your Presence. Ask for an idea or inspiration to come to you, as you open, listen and wait. Jot down anything that comes to you—anything

CHAPTER SEVEN

THE GOLDEN RULE REVISED

I LEARNED THE GOLDEN RULE as a young child, in the context of my Christian upbringing. I was taught, "Do unto others as you would have them do unto you." I took it to mean, "Be nice." Treat others in the same way you want to be treated. It also might be interpreted to mean, love others in the way you want to be loved, or even, act in the same way you'd like others to act. Have you ever noticed this is harder than it seems?

We all know how to be friendly and kind, but have you ever found yourself being mean or rejecting to someone who has hurt you? Have you ever talked behind someone's back when other friends were gossiping, or lied to someone you love because you didn't want them to judge you? We all have pushed away our parents and siblings with anger and dismissed people we didn't trust or like. Sometimes we act in ways that surprise us. "That's not like me," we think. Our hearts aren't always as open and loving as we want them to be, and let's face it, we don't always treat others in the ways we want to be treated. Why not?

The answer is complicated and has many moving pieces, but one reason is because we have defensive, skeptical parts of us that block our best Self. The function of these parts is to hide our vulnerabilities, and offer instead, extreme beliefs and emotions that defend against further hurts. These parts blame others and make us feel victimized or unfairly treated. They serve to protect us with rigid strategies, and prevent us from living with an open, trusting heart. We begin to see the world through the eyes of caution. We begin to close off from others, feeling more and more separate as we pull back, and focus on differences rather than similarities. We don't take the time to listen and understand. We just see people through the lens of the past. The irony is, the relationship and attitudes we have toward others are merely a reflection of the relationship we have with ourselves.

For most of us, the relationship we have with ourselves is, at best, fickle. Many of us set the bar pretty high, and our "blamer part" often turns its scorn around toward us if we don't meet certain expectations. We have competitive parts that want to win, be the best, always succeed, and do it all, yet when faced with our human limitations, we judge ourselves harshly. After years of making mistakes and coming up short when compared to the abilities and accomplishments of others, it's easy to conclude we're not good enough. We develop a loud critical voice within us, who always lets us know how we should have said it differently or done it better. We also may have a guilty part that causes us regret and shame. As we give over our higher, wiser perspective to these parts of us, we develop inner conflicts which disrupt our ability to be kind and compassionate with others.

The parts of us we hate, hide, criticize, and exile are the traits we hate or fear in others. We can't be open hearted to others because we aren't open to ourselves. We can't trust others because we are deceiving ourselves. We focus on the faults of others as a defense, to keep our awareness away from our own weaknesses. We fear the judgement of others because our own self-criticism is so tough. As long as we find fault with ourselves, we will never be able to follow the Golden Rule. We can only be as kind and compassionate to others as we can be toward ourselves. Therefore, my variation of the Golden Rule is, "Do unto thyself as you would have others do unto you." Or, "Treat *yourself* in the same way you want others to treat you."

Self-Inquiry Practice for Internal Kindness:
What stops you from loving yourself? Are there parts of you that sometimes feel hard to like or even control? Do some of them take you over, influencing your behavior with extreme emotion? Are you aware of other parts that try to numb or cool those big emotions with food, alcohol, or spending money? Is there a part that is self-righteous? Holding strong and rigid beliefs? Can you be open and curious? Listen compassionately to these parts to learn of their back-story and motivation? What do they want for you? How can you win their trust and respect, and still remain the leader of your system?

CHAPTER EIGHT

BRINGING TRUE-SELF LEADERSHIP INTO THE WORLD:

Loving and Leading from the Inside Out

IF WE RELATE MY "REVISED GOLDEN RULE" to the concepts of love and leadership, we could say, "Love yourself in the ways you want to be loved, lead in the ways you want to be led."

It seems especially important in this current time of social/political division and unrest for each of us to do our own personal healing work and lead ourselves with more mindful, compassionate awareness, before we fight against the actions or opinions of others. As we aim toward a transformed society which prioritizes integrity, mutual respect, equality, harmony, and freedom, we must first offer these things to ourselves. As we ask elected officials and those in authority to act in accordance with our highest values, we need to keep a close eye on our own level of integrity and self-respect. We must not defer our personal responsibility to inspire and lead *each other*, by example, in our day-to-day lives. We need to examine our expectations for ourselves as well as for our leaders with the same standards, clarity, and awareness. Hating and blaming the "other" might just be a projection of how we hate, blame, and exile parts of ourselves that have become extreme and harmful.

Wise community leadership can facilitate a reasonable amount of balance, cooperation, and positive direction, despite an environment of diversity and difference, which we need to always welcome. But, this balance must first exist within the leader. A habit of Self-awareness and Self-Leadership allows an open, respectful, global view of how best to lead others with integrity and transparency. It is not too idealistic to believe that we *can* be the kind friend, collaborative co-worker, tireless community volunteer, understanding parent, forgiving child, or inspirational leader without fear or selfish motives, if we make internal space for the intelligence of our true nature. From the love and higher wisdom of our true Self, we can connect with and lead people in a way that benefits all of us, with the goal of cooperation and collaboration.

This is a powerful time of change. There is a cultural shift beginning to occur, propelled by the desire for truth, accountability and mutual respect. As we face constant exposure of the ugly realities of injustice, corruption, and abuse of power, our determination grows. These patterns of aggression and imbalance need to be acknowledged and corrected. As we learn to develop a transparency within ourselves, we then have more clarity regarding how we contribute to the problems of our society. As we see the pain in ourselves, we can see the pain in others. As we grow to understand that we *all* share in the experience of human suffering, we begin to feel our similarities rather than our differences. The true Self in all of us is connected to and resourced from the same universal wisdom and love that is beyond our human understanding.

With intention, we can open up to this connective Energy—a Presence that provides us more possibilities for creative solutions.

At this stage of our evolution, as we consider the possibility of the world's problems as representative of the inner conflicts, extreme beliefs, and pain within our own human hearts, can we begin asking tough questions with a curious, open mind? Have I been born into privilege? Have I been born into conflict, struggle, and burden? How have both men and women been hurt as children? And, how have they been taught to act? What are the cultural expectations that pressure us? What are the messages we have received about power, race, sexuality, prejudice, anger, duty, strength, tolerance, and identity?

Are we ready to heal ourselves, individually? Are we even familiar with the inner pathways that lead to transformation, and are we ready to explore these deeper places within? Are we willing to see the ugly, the painful, the shameful within ourselves and know these extremes are just results of being hurt while living this human life? Can we forgive ourselves for our imperfections and mistakes? Most importantly, can we be courageous enough to be curious about whatever we find, and open ourselves with compassion, so that we can then be a channel for greater peace and creative collaboration in the world? Richard Schwartz, founder of the IFS framework believes that for each of us, at our essence is pure peace and joy, and from this place we are able to sense spiritual connectedness and manifest leadership qualities that are reparative.

For those involved with social activism, I support you and thank you. You are the voice of change. I invite you to lovingly stay connected to your internal world, being as curious as possible. Remember to be aware of your deeper mind and heart, and check for exhaustion, despair, grief, and old wounds carried by parts of you that need your compassionate attention. With discernment, be clear about the source of your drive, and the power of your anger. These are to be honored, without allowing extreme emotions to lead to aggression and hatred. Keep turning within. Just notice which part of you is leading. What's the deeper agenda? What is underneath? Is the agenda driven by pain? Is your pain impeding the higher wisdom, power, and perspective of your wisest Self, the ultimate leader? Notice, too, if there's a part of you that reacts to these questions. Do you feel resistance toward becoming curious and still? Try not to judge any part of you. All parts are welcome and need your compassionate connection in order for you to be the powerful change-agent the world needs.

As we listen to parts that won't let go, hijacking us with pain, grief, powerlessness, or anger, our aim is not to get rid of them. We merely need to listen, comfort, and get to know their dynamics. We do this so they feel heard, seen, and appreciated in a way that cannot be done by someone in the outer world. We are all personally responsible for understanding and transforming our own emotional wounds. This job does not belong to anyone but ourselves, and it cannot depend on the world changing around us. We must create the change, starting from within. By connecting to yourself—to your own inner world, you are able then, to enter the outer world with more confident Presence, and a charismatic leadership that is hard for the world to deny. You become empowered to create the impact that you desire.

Again, this healing connection you provide *yourself* is deeper and more powerful than any act of love, protection, or emotional support you can receive from someone else. Your attitude of unconditional love for *yourself* can change everything... It satisfies the deep longing for the connectedness we all seek from others. It allows a higher intelligence and vision to flow through you, inspiring you in a natural way. To experience the depth, power, and sweetness of your own divine essence is the fullness which allows you to live and love generously and lead compassionately, with the open-hearted awareness of your true Self. This is how we change the world, loving and leading from the inside out.

A special note to therapists, coaches, teachers, clergy, administrators, mediators, and anyone else who will teach this to others, please take this truth to heart: As we offer this model to the people we work with, it is crucially important that we do our *own, ongoing* work. We cannot help, teach, or ask this of others if we cannot come from an authentic place of experiential knowing of what this process is like. It will be ineffective to ask someone to speak for an angry manager part if our own part, which disapproves of anger, won't relax back, allowing our true Self to be there. If we cannot listen to and lead our own parts, they will definitely interject their interpretations. It will be difficult to hear someone expressing the painful emotions of their exiled part, if we do not know how to deal with our own. Exiles tend to trigger each other, and this phenomenon adds a special challenge when we are trying to hold our highest perspective.

If we continue to believe that it is *our* skill, or technique, or even our Self-Energy that is the change-agent, we will forever feel responsible, become burned out, and never know the truth, which is the fact that it is the Self-Energy in those we work with that does the work. It is our job to empower people to turn inward to meet their own resourceful and brilliant system. It is only our own experience of Self, and our ability to hold this Energy with others that allows a mutually beneficial connection. Consider finding your own IFS consultant or therapist. It will make a huge difference.

CHAPTER NINE

INSTRUCTIONS FOR THE SELF-INQUIRY TRACKING (SIT) PROCESS

THE IMPORTANCE OF OUR COMMITMENT to a daily self-inquiry practice cannot be overstated, if we want to love and lead in a different way. We know this is a time of imbalance, and we cannot solve our problems at the psychological level at which they have occurred. For us to advance our consciousness and our ability to live together on a thriving planet, we need to expand our own sense of spiritual greatness. We need to prioritize a practice, any practice, of finding that calm open space within us that can serve as our greatest resource. Some time spent in quiet connection with your Self and with whatever part of you needs attention, will open up mental and emotional space within you. From this space comes the valuable gifts of peace, awareness, clarity, intelligence, confidence, compassion etc. Your mind can feel more like a friend than an enemy.

The most challenging part of the six-step Self-Inquiry Tracking (SIT) process is staying devoted to your practice. Your intention needs to be set now, to complete thiry SIT sheets before you give up and do something else. Then, your intention needs to be set again each night, to get the sleep you need so that you can rise earlier than you'd like. Though it is different for everyone, it usually takes about twenty to thirty minutes to complete the process. Your busy mind, daily schedule, fast lifestyle, or family demands, along with your action-driven parts, may *not* support you, but do it anyway. Observing your mind and all its parts, and building a better relationship with yourself is *at least* as useful as anything else you do, and in fact may enhance every other aspect of your life.

The following explanations describe the six steps of the Self-Inquiry Tracking (SIT) process. Refer to these often until the process becomes natural. There are thirty sheets for your use at the end of this guidebook. Let them be a journal and a testament to your growth and healing over the next thirty days. At the end of each, on the back of each sheet is space for you to map out your inner parts, and note their various perspectives and dialogue as you become aware of them.

Step 1: Center
To begin the SIT process, find a comfortable place to sit. Let go of the outer world and its distractions, but do not push away any thoughts or emotions you may be having. To "center," just draw your attention inward, and focus on your breathing. Do this for eight to ten breaths or for about one minute. As you focus, notice the pace and depth of your breathing, and the degree of ease from inhale to exhale. Set your intention to be patient and as attentive as possible. Keep this step short and deliberate. This is not a time to meditate. It's a time to switch your attention from the outer world to your inner world, and pay attention. Begin to welcome any parts of you to come forward.

INSTRUCTIONS FOR THE SELF-INQUIRY TRACKING (SIT) PROCESS

Step 2: Notice
This is the step where you aim for non-judgmental mindfulness—an awareness of what you are experiencing. After focusing your attention on your breathing for a minute or two, your mind will probably begin to wander, thinking about other things. Can you notice what those are? How do you feel, emotionally? Do you notice any sensations in your body, like tension, pain, or restlessness? Invite all thoughts, feelings, and sensations to be there. They are probably related to each other. Be curious, and do not breathe or meditate them away! The goal here is not to ignore or become distracted by what you notice, just merely make note of it all, without judgement or, notice the judgement and be curious about *that!* If your mind sounds so noisy and seems too chaotic to identify any one particular thought or emotion, know that it's very common. Just make note of it. Perhaps experiment a little and ask your parts to slow down so you can notice them. See what happens.

After you have noted your thoughts, feelings, and body sensations, see if you can name the part of you that is making you feel/think all this. (e.g the Worrier, the Analyst, the Critic etc.) Then answer the questions listed under Step Two.

Step 3: Listen
This is the step where you access your curiosity to get to know the part and befriend it, just like you would in a new relationship. You want to be really open and curious, even if it's a part that hijacks you in a negative way. Hopefully you can feel some compassion toward it, after understanding it better. To do this, just answer the questions, listed in Step Three. Then set your intention for the day. If, for example, you notice in Step Two a part that is carrying anger and resentment, but you really want to find space in your heart for the calm and compassion (aspects of your Self-Energy) that are needed for balance,

then set that intention as your focus for the day, asking your parts to open space for these qualities (Step Four).

Step 4: Negotiate/Ask
This is the step of Self-Leadership, where you kindly guide and lead your parts, asking for their cooperation. First, hold in mind your intention for the day. Repeat it to your parts. Then begin to lead your system by following the steps of negotiation and awareness.

Step 5: Open/Own It:
This is the step that most closely resembles meditation. It's when you take a few minutes to rest in the open spaciousness of your own being. This step can be done in silence, or while listening to the corresponding meditation, offered on the CD or Mp3 recording, *Meditations for Self-Awareness and Self-Leadership* (available at www.holisticcounselwny.com). Follow the instructions listed for this step, resting in the awareness of your True-Self Presence. Breathe, and allow your chosen Self-Energy qualities to emerge naturally. Your parts do not have to manufacture this experience. They just need to allow it to happen.

Step 6: Remember/Reinforce:
Whenever we try to develop a new habit, we need to remember what we're doing and reinforce it. Your ability to lead your system and maintain your intention will not always be easy. Parts of you may resist, stressful things will happen during the day, and your parts will get triggered, obscuring your Presence. It's important to manage your time during the day so that you can have a few quiet moments to check-in. Create a plan to remember, cultivate, and reinforce your chosen Self-Energy quality. Take time to be outside in nature or in a quiet indoor space. Set an alarm or write a reminder on your phone of your intention.

INSTRUCTIONS FOR THE SELF-INQUIRY TRACKING (SIT) PROCESS

Evening Reflections (Optional):
Although this step is optional, it is very useful. It's an opportunity to reconnect with your parts, checking in to see if there are any parts that need your attention. At the end of the day, ask yourself, "How did the day go? Was I aware? What parts got triggered? Did I bring compassion and appreciation to all parts? Are there any parts who still need my attention?" If so, befriend them. If your inner critic is being harsh because you completely forgot about your intention, then just be with that part, in a compassionate way.

After doing this process for a few days, you will get the hang of it. Additionally, it might be helpful for you to practice and share your insights with an IFS life coach or therapist. You can find someone local, to see in person, or work with online by going to: www.selfleadership.org. Please seek out professional help if you have traumatic memories or extreme parts that disturb you. Sometimes we need the support of someone else's Self-Energy to help us along the path of transformation.

The following pages consist of thirty SIT journal sheets for you to complete in the next five weeks. Remember to keep it simple, watching out for any perfectionist parts! If it takes too long, you'll most likely drop it, so just show up each day for as long as you can, and trust your process. Hopefully you will find your own rhythm, and you can eventually continue doing it on your own, beyond the thirty days, with a regular journal, or without any prompting at all. My hope is that the process of self-inquiry becomes a habit that grows organically within you, as you need it. As you develop this habit, I invite you to notice how the eight Cs begin to show up, more and more in your work and relationships. I offer you my warmest wishes for a rewarding exploration of continued *Self*-discovery and *Self*-Leadership!

AFTERWORD

TRUE SELF-LEADERSHIP CAN HELP us practice a new way of being human; to be kinder, more authentic, honest, trusting, caring, innovative and powerful. We can gain a broader view and be more accountable, acting from our highest, best Self. We can learn to unburden our pain with Self-compassion and inner connection so that we no longer bring it into the world. We can feel safer being honest and open, more discerning in our choices, as we aim toward peace rather than conflict and division.

I now realize that those thousands of Wyoming stars were not just representing opportunities and choices that impact my existence in the external world, but more importantly, they symbolize all opportunities I have to positively impact my internal world. The choices that we make every day about our thoughts, speech and actions, our focus, our priorities, and our relationship to ourselves determine the depth and meaning of our life experience. How do we spend our precious time? Who do we spend it with? What toxic information and energy are we allowing into our field of awareness? What do we do to renew and heal? How do we talk to ourselves? Can we be more mindful

AFTERWORD

in noticing our decisions? Are we living and loving deliberately? Can we be curious?

I invite you to create and follow your own journey toward connection through mindful Self-Inquiry. Discover SIT as a loving practice of opening your heart and mind. If this practice isn't for you, toss it. But, find another one that interests you, and commit to it. Do little things throughout the day which allow experiences of joy and alignment with your true Self. Experience the subtle energies of nature, that underlie its form and beauty. Find things to appreciate about your life. Rely only on the wisdom you find within. Your only master is you. You can trust the love and wisdom of your true Self, to bring goodness, naturally, to the people and places where it is most needed.

Walk a little slower. Breathe a little deeper. Live more deliberately. Take a longer look at the person in front of you. You are deeply connected, sharing in the mystery, joy, and suffering of being human. Embrace your story. And, embrace those of others. Turn up the corners of your mouth and find your inner smile, while you sit and just be. You are good enough. Feel the calm stillness between your breaths. And, let it all unfold...

As you bring your true Self into the world, sharing your gifts, I will meet you there.

Self-Inquiry Tracking (SIT) Journal Sheet   Date _____

1. Center: Focus on the flow of your breathing. Don't clear away your thoughts. Just be aware...

2. Notice: What's on your mind? List prominent thoughts/emotions/sensations. Name the part.

Thoughts ——>   Emotions ——>   Bodily Sensations ——>   Name of Part

Ask yourself: "How do I *feel toward* this part of me?" _____
"Can I be curious, compassionate or nonjudgmental?" _____
If so, go to Step Three. If not, you have another part blocking your Self-Energy. Be inquisitive about the interference. What's it about? _____.
After listening, kindly ask the interfering part to relax and allow you to be more open and present. If the resistance won't relax, do Step Three with the resistant part. If the resistance relaxes, you can continue, focusing on the part you originally noticed.

3. Listen: In a neutral, curious way, get to know the part of you identified in Step Two. Ask whatever questions you are curious about, such as:

     a). What is your purpose (or job) within my system? _____
     b). *How* do you do your job? _____
     c). How long have you been doing this, and what is it like for you to have this job? _____
     _____
     d). What are you afraid will happen if you stop doing your job? _____
     e). What are you protecting? _____

Again, ask: "How am I feeling toward this part, now?" _____.
Tell the part. Ask other parts to soften if they interfere with your Self-Energy, e.g. compassion.

Set your intentions: Listen to your deepest impulse, and be aware of how you would authentically like to feel, if you weren't under the influence of this part. Choose the Self-Energy quality, below, that matches how you *want* to be today, in contrast to what you noticed in Step Two. Circle it below and set your intention to cultivate and hold this quality today, being aware of and manager parts that try to take over. For example: "Today I want to feel my innate confidence. I open to my confidence as the core of my being." Write your intention: _____
_____

Calm   Curiosity   Connectedness   Clarity   Compassion   Courage   Confidence   Creativity

4. Negotiate/Ask: Repeat your intention silently to your parts. Then begin leading your system of parts, asking for their cooperation:

a). Negotiate this plan by first asking the parts if they notice you and how much you care. If so, ask if they would relax, trust you, and open space for you to be Present.

They do not need to force or make this happen. They can relax while you open.

b). Be aware of (and name) any parts that resist the plan, listen to their perspectives, and keep on negotiating with them.*

5. Open/Own It: When you feel a sense of permission, get centered again by focusing on the flow of your breath, relax, and bring your fullest attention to the present moment. Find stillness. Rest there. Allow calm to arise, first. Feel your Presence. Breathe and allow your chosen quality (or others) to emerge naturally. Feel it in your body. Envision yourself being this way throughout your day. Own it. Allow it to resonate as your true, essential nature.**

Notes: _____

_____

6. Remember/Reinforce: Create a plan to remember and cultivate your chosen Self-Energy quality for today. Set alarms or reminders on your phone, naming your quality, plan pleasant activities, be aware of obstacles presented by oppositional parts. My plan for today includes:

_____

_____

Evening Reflections: How did the day go? Was I aware? What parts got triggered? Did I bring compassion-appreciation to all parts? Are there any parts who still need my attention? If so, befriend them. Notes: _____

* If you have difficulty getting beyond this point, seek support from an IFS professional. The resistance is a healing opportunity, not a failure. Never push away a part. All parts are welcome.

** The recording; Meditations for Self-Awareness and Self-Leadership aligns with and supports this process. To order, go to www.holisticcounselwny.com, and download more SIT Sheets for free.

Additional Notes or Parts Mapping:

Self-Inquiry Tracking (SIT) Journal Sheet   Date _____

1. Center: Focus on the flow of your breathing. Don't clear away your thoughts. Just be aware…

2. Notice: What's on your mind? List prominent thoughts/emotions/sensations. Name the part.

Thoughts ——> Emotions ——> Bodily Sensations ——> Name of Part

Ask yourself: "How do I *feel toward* this part of me?" _____
"Can I be curious, compassionate or nonjudgmental?" _____
If so, go to Step Three. If not, you have another part blocking your Self-Energy. Be inquisitive about the interference. What's it about? _____.
After listening, kindly ask the interfering part to relax and allow you to be more open and present. If the resistance won't relax, do Step Three with the resistant part. If the resistance relaxes, you can continue, focusing on the part you originally noticed.

3. Listen: In a neutral, curious way, get to know the part of you identified in Step Two. Ask whatever questions you are curious about, such as:
   a). What is your purpose (or job) within my system? _____
   b). *How* do you do your job? _____
   c). How long have you been doing this, and what is it like for you to have this job? _____
   _____
   d). What are you afraid will happen if you stop doing your job? _____
   e). What are you protecting? _____

Again, ask: "How am I feeling toward this part, now?" _____.
Tell the part. Ask other parts to soften if they interfere with your Self-Energy, e.g. compassion.

Set your intentions: Listen to your deepest impulse, and be aware of how you would authentically like to feel, if you weren't under the influence of this part. Choose the Self-Energy quality, below, that matches how you *want* to be today, in contrast to what you noticed in Step Two. Circle it below and set your intention to cultivate and hold this quality today, being aware of and manager parts that try to take over. For example: "Today I want to feel my innate confidence. I open to my confidence as the core of my being." Write your intention: _____
_____

Calm   Curiosity   Connectedness   Clarity   Compassion   Courage   Confidence   Creativity

4. Negotiate/Ask: Repeat your intention silently to your parts. Then begin leading your system of parts, asking for their cooperation:

a). Negotiate this plan by first asking the parts if they notice you and how much you care. If so, ask if they would relax, trust you, and open space for you to be Present.

They do not need to force or make this happen. They can relax while you open.

b). Be aware of (and name) any parts that resist the plan, listen to their perspectives, and keep on negotiating with them.*

5. Open/Own It: When you feel a sense of permission, get centered again by focusing on the flow of your breath, relax, and bring your fullest attention to the present moment. Find stillness. Rest there. Allow calm to arise, first. Feel your Presence. Breathe and allow your chosen quality (or others) to emerge naturally. Feel it in your body. Envision yourself being this way throughout your day. Own it. Allow it to resonate as your true, essential nature.**
Notes: _____
_____

6. Remember/Reinforce: Create a plan to remember and cultivate your chosen Self-Energy quality for today. Set alarms or reminders on your phone, naming your quality, plan pleasant activities, be aware of obstacles presented by oppositional parts. My plan for today includes:
_____
_____

Evening Reflections: How did the day go? Was I aware? What parts got triggered? Did I bring compassion-appreciation to all parts? Are there any parts who still need my attention? If so, befriend them. Notes: _____

* If you have difficulty getting beyond this point, seek support from an IFS professional. The resistance is a healing opportunity, not a failure. Never push away a part. All parts are welcome.

** The recording; Meditations for Self-Awareness and Self-Leadership aligns with and supports this process. To order, go to www.holisticcounselwny.com, and download more SIT Sheets for free.

Additional Notes or Parts Mapping:

Self-Inquiry Tracking (SIT) Journal Sheet   Date _____

1. Center: Focus on the flow of your breathing. Don't clear away your thoughts. Just be aware…

2. Notice: What's on your mind? List prominent thoughts/emotions/sensations. Name the part.

Thoughts ——> Emotions ——> Bodily Sensations ——> Name of Part

Ask yourself: "How do I *feel toward* this part of me?" _____
"Can I be curious, compassionate or nonjudgmental?" _____
If so, go to Step Three. If not, you have another part blocking your Self-Energy. Be inquisitive about the interference. What's it about? _____.
After listening, kindly ask the interfering part to relax and allow you to be more open and present. If the resistance won't relax, do Step Three with the resistant part. If the resistance relaxes, you can continue, focusing on the part you originally noticed.

3. Listen: In a neutral, curious way, get to know the part of you identified in Step Two. Ask whatever questions you are curious about, such as:

   a). What is your purpose (or job) within my system? _____
   b). *How* do you do your job? _____
   c). How long have you been doing this, and what is it like for you to have this job? _____
   _____
   d). What are you afraid will happen if you stop doing your job? _____
   e). What are you protecting? _____

Again, ask: "How am I feeling toward this part, now?" _____.
Tell the part. Ask other parts to soften if they interfere with your Self-Energy, e.g. compassion.

Set your intentions: Listen to your deepest impulse, and be aware of how you would authentically like to feel, if you weren't under the influence of this part. Choose the Self-Energy quality, below, that matches how you *want* to be today, in contrast to what you noticed in Step Two. Circle it below and set your intention to cultivate and hold this quality today, being aware of and manager parts that try to take over. For example: "Today I want to feel my innate confidence. I open to my confidence as the core of my being." Write your intention: _____
_____

Calm   Curiosity   Connectedness   Clarity   Compassion   Courage   Confidence   Creativity

4. Negotiate/Ask: Repeat your intention silently to your parts. Then begin leading your system of parts, asking for their cooperation:

a). Negotiate this plan by first asking the parts if they notice you and how much you care. If so, ask if they would relax, trust you, and open space for you to be Present.

They do not need to force or make this happen. They can relax while you open.

b). Be aware of (and name) any parts that resist the plan, listen to their perspectives, and keep on negotiating with them.*

5. Open/Own It: When you feel a sense of permission, get centered again by focusing on the flow of your breath, relax, and bring your fullest attention to the present moment. Find stillness. Rest there. Allow calm to arise, first. Feel your Presence. Breathe and allow your chosen quality (or others) to emerge naturally. Feel it in your body. Envision yourself being this way throughout your day. Own it. Allow it to resonate as your true, essential nature.**

Notes: _____

_____

6. Remember/Reinforce: Create a plan to remember and cultivate your chosen Self-Energy quality for today. Set alarms or reminders on your phone, naming your quality, plan pleasant activities, be aware of obstacles presented by oppositional parts. My plan for today includes:

_____

_____

Evening Reflections: How did the day go? Was I aware? What parts got triggered? Did I bring compassion-appreciation to all parts? Are there any parts who still need my attention? If so, befriend them. Notes: _____

* If you have difficulty getting beyond this point, seek support from an IFS professional. The resistance is a healing opportunity, not a failure. Never push away a part. All parts are welcome.

** The recording; Meditations for Self-Awareness and Self-Leadership aligns with and supports this process. To order, go to www.holisticcounselwny.com, and download more SIT Sheets for free.

Additional Notes or Parts Mapping:

Self-Inquiry Tracking (SIT) Journal Sheet   Date _____

1. Center: Focus on the flow of your breathing. Don't clear away your thoughts. Just be aware…

2. Notice: What's on your mind? List prominent thoughts/emotions/sensations. Name the part.

Thoughts ———> Emotions ———> Bodily Sensations ———> Name of Part

Ask yourself: "How do I *feel toward* this part of me?" _____
"Can I be curious, compassionate or nonjudgmental?" _____
If so, go to Step Three. If not, you have another part blocking your Self-Energy. Be inquisitive about the interference. What's it about? _____.
After listening, kindly ask the interfering part to relax and allow you to be more open and present. If the resistance won't relax, do Step Three with the resistant part. If the resistance relaxes, you can continue, focusing on the part you originally noticed.

3. Listen: In a neutral, curious way, get to know the part of you identified in Step Two. Ask whatever questions you are curious about, such as:

    a). What is your purpose (or job) within my system? _____
    b). *How* do you do your job? _____
    c). How long have you been doing this, and what is it like for you to have this job? _____
    _____
    d). What are you afraid will happen if you stop doing your job? _____
    e). What are you protecting? _____

Again, ask: "How am I feeling toward this part, now?" _____.
Tell the part. Ask other parts to soften if they interfere with your Self-Energy, e.g. compassion.

Set your intentions: Listen to your deepest impulse, and be aware of how you would authentically like to feel, if you weren't under the influence of this part. Choose the Self-Energy quality, below, that matches how you *want* to be today, in contrast to what you noticed in Step Two. Circle it below and set your intention to cultivate and hold this quality today, being aware of and manager parts that try to take over. For example: "Today I want to feel my innate confidence. I open to my confidence as the core of my being." Write your intention: _____
_____

Calm   Curiosity   Connectedness   Clarity   Compassion   Courage   Confidence   Creativity

4. Negotiate/Ask: Repeat your intention silently to your parts. Then begin leading your system of parts, asking for their cooperation:

    a). Negotiate this plan by first asking the parts if they notice you and how much you care. If so, ask if they would relax, trust you, and open space for you to be Present.

        They do not need to force or make this happen. They can relax while you open.

    b). Be aware of (and name) any parts that resist the plan, listen to their perspectives, and keep on negotiating with them.*

5. Open/Own It: When you feel a sense of permission, get centered again by focusing on the flow of your breath, relax, and bring your fullest attention to the present moment. Find stillness. Rest there. Allow calm to arise, first. Feel your Presence. Breathe and allow your chosen quality (or others) to emerge naturally. Feel it in your body. Envision yourself being this way throughout your day. Own it. Allow it to resonate as your true, essential nature.**

Notes: _____

_____

6. Remember/Reinforce: Create a plan to remember and cultivate your chosen Self-Energy quality for today. Set alarms or reminders on your phone, naming your quality, plan pleasant activities, be aware of obstacles presented by oppositional parts. My plan for today includes:

_____

_____

Evening Reflections: How did the day go? Was I aware? What parts got triggered? Did I bring compassion-appreciation to all parts? Are there any parts who still need my attention? If so, befriend them. Notes: _____

* If you have difficulty getting beyond this point, seek support from an IFS professional. The resistance is a healing opportunity, not a failure. Never push away a part. All parts are welcome.

** The recording; Meditations for Self-Awareness and Self-Leadership aligns with and supports this process. To order, go to www.holisticcounselwny.com, and download more SIT Sheets for free.

Additional Notes or Parts Mapping:

Self-Inquiry Tracking (SIT) Journal Sheet   Date _____

1. Center: Focus on the flow of your breathing. Don't clear away your thoughts. Just be aware…

2. Notice: What's on your mind? List prominent thoughts/emotions/sensations. Name the part.

Thoughts   ——>   Emotions   ——>   Bodily Sensations   ——>   Name of Part

Ask yourself: "How do I *feel toward* this part of me?" _____
"Can I be curious, compassionate or nonjudgmental?" _____
If so, go to Step Three. If not, you have another part blocking your Self-Energy. Be inquisitive about the interference. What's it about? _____.
After listening, kindly ask the interfering part to relax and allow you to be more open and present. If the resistance won't relax, do Step Three with the resistant part. If the resistance relaxes, you can continue, focusing on the part you originally noticed.

3. Listen: In a neutral, curious way, get to know the part of you identified in Step Two. Ask whatever questions you are curious about, such as:

   a). What is your purpose (or job) within my system? _____
   b). *How* do you do your job? _____
   c). How long have you been doing this, and what is it like for you to have this job? _____
   _____
   d). What are you afraid will happen if you stop doing your job? _____
   e). What are you protecting? _____

Again, ask: "How am I feeling toward this part, now?" _____.
Tell the part. Ask other parts to soften if they interfere with your Self-Energy, e.g. compassion.

Set your intentions: Listen to your deepest impulse, and be aware of how you would authentically like to feel, if you weren't under the influence of this part. Choose the Self-Energy quality, below, that matches how you *want* to be today, in contrast to what you noticed in Step Two. Circle it below and set your intention to cultivate and hold this quality today, being aware of and manager parts that try to take over. For example: "Today I want to feel my innate confidence. I open to my confidence as the core of my being." Write your intention: _____
_____

Calm   Curiosity   Connectedness   Clarity   Compassion   Courage   Confidence   Creativity

4. Negotiate/Ask: Repeat your intention silently to your parts. Then begin leading your system of parts, asking for their cooperation:

a). Negotiate this plan by first asking the parts if they notice you and how much you care. If so, ask if they would relax, trust you, and open space for you to be Present.

They do not need to force or make this happen. They can relax while you open.

b). Be aware of (and name) any parts that resist the plan, listen to their perspectives, and keep on negotiating with them.*

5. Open/Own It: When you feel a sense of permission, get centered again by focusing on the flow of your breath, relax, and bring your fullest attention to the present moment. Find stillness. Rest there. Allow calm to arise, first. Feel your Presence. Breathe and allow your chosen quality (or others) to emerge naturally. Feel it in your body. Envision yourself being this way throughout your day. Own it. Allow it to resonate as your true, essential nature.**

Notes: _____

_____

6. Remember/Reinforce: Create a plan to remember and cultivate your chosen Self-Energy quality for today. Set alarms or reminders on your phone, naming your quality, plan pleasant activities, be aware of obstacles presented by oppositional parts. My plan for today includes:

_____

_____

Evening Reflections: How did the day go? Was I aware? What parts got triggered? Did I bring compassion-appreciation to all parts? Are there any parts who still need my attention? If so, befriend them. Notes: _____

* If you have difficulty getting beyond this point, seek support from an IFS professional. The resistance is a healing opportunity, not a failure. Never push away a part. All parts are welcome.

** The recording; Meditations for Self-Awareness and Self-Leadership aligns with and supports this process. To order, go to www.holisticcounselwny.com, and download more SIT Sheets for free.

Additional Notes or Parts Mapping:

Self-Inquiry Tracking (SIT) Journal Sheet   Date _____

1. Center: Focus on the flow of your breathing. Don't clear away your thoughts. Just be aware...

2. Notice: What's on your mind? List prominent thoughts/emotions/sensations. Name the part.

Thoughts   ——>   Emotions   ——>   Bodily Sensations   ——>   Name of Part

Ask yourself: "How do I *feel toward* this part of me?" _____
"Can I be curious, compassionate or nonjudgmental?" _____
If so, go to Step Three. If not, you have another part blocking your Self-Energy. Be inquisitive about the interference. What's it about? _____.
After listening, kindly ask the interfering part to relax and allow you to be more open and present. If the resistance won't relax, do Step Three with the resistant part. If the resistance relaxes, you can continue, focusing on the part you originally noticed.

3. Listen: In a neutral, curious way, get to know the part of you identified in Step Two. Ask whatever questions you are curious about, such as:
    a). What is your purpose (or job) within my system? _____
    b). *How* do you do your job? _____
    c). How long have you been doing this, and what is it like for you to have this job? _____
    _____
    d). What are you afraid will happen if you stop doing your job? _____
    e). What are you protecting? _____

Again, ask: "How am I feeling toward this part, now?" _____.
Tell the part. Ask other parts to soften if they interfere with your Self-Energy, e.g. compassion.

Set your intentions: Listen to your deepest impulse, and be aware of how you would authentically like to feel, if you weren't under the influence of this part. Choose the Self-Energy quality, below, that matches how you *want* to be today, in contrast to what you noticed in Step Two. Circle it below and set your intention to cultivate and hold this quality today, being aware of and manager parts that try to take over. For example: "Today I want to feel my innate confidence. I open to my confidence as the core of my being." Write your intention: _____
_____

Calm   Curiosity   Connectedness   Clarity   Compassion   Courage   Confidence   Creativity

4. Negotiate/Ask: Repeat your intention silently to your parts. Then begin leading your system of parts, asking for their cooperation:

    a). Negotiate this plan by first asking the parts if they notice you and how much you care. If so, ask if they would relax, trust you, and open space for you to be Present.

        They do not need to force or make this happen. They can relax while you open.

    b). Be aware of (and name) any parts that resist the plan, listen to their perspectives, and keep on negotiating with them.*

5. Open/Own It: When you feel a sense of permission, get centered again by focusing on the flow of your breath, relax, and bring your fullest attention to the present moment. Find stillness. Rest there. Allow calm to arise, first. Feel your Presence. Breathe and allow your chosen quality (or others) to emerge naturally. Feel it in your body. Envision yourself being this way throughout your day. Own it. Allow it to resonate as your true, essential nature.**

Notes: _____

_____

6. Remember/Reinforce: Create a plan to remember and cultivate your chosen Self-Energy quality for today. Set alarms or reminders on your phone, naming your quality, plan pleasant activities, be aware of obstacles presented by oppositional parts. My plan for today includes:

_____

_____

Evening Reflections: How did the day go? Was I aware? What parts got triggered? Did I bring compassion-appreciation to all parts? Are there any parts who still need my attention? If so, befriend them. Notes: _____

* If you have difficulty getting beyond this point, seek support from an IFS professional. The resistance is a healing opportunity, not a failure. Never push away a part. All parts are welcome.

** The recording; Meditations for Self-Awareness and Self-Leadership aligns with and supports this process. To order, go to www.holisticcounselwny.com, and download more SIT Sheets for free.

Additional Notes or Parts Mapping:

Self-Inquiry Tracking (SIT) Journal Sheet   Date _____

1. Center: Focus on the flow of your breathing. Don't clear away your thoughts. Just be aware...

2. Notice: What's on your mind? List prominent thoughts/emotions/sensations. Name the part.

Thoughts   ——>   Emotions   ——>   Bodily Sensations   ——>   Name of Part

Ask yourself: "How do I *feel toward* this part of me?" _____
"Can I be curious, compassionate or nonjudgmental?" _____
If so, go to Step Three. If not, you have another part blocking your Self-Energy. Be inquisitive about the interference. What's it about? _____.
After listening, kindly ask the interfering part to relax and allow you to be more open and present. If the resistance won't relax, do Step Three with the resistant part. If the resistance relaxes, you can continue, focusing on the part you originally noticed.

3. Listen: In a neutral, curious way, get to know the part of you identified in Step Two. Ask whatever questions you are curious about, such as:

    a). What is your purpose (or job) within my system? _____
    b). *How* do you do your job? _____
    c). How long have you been doing this, and what is it like for you to have this job? _____
_____
    d). What are you afraid will happen if you stop doing your job? _____
    e). What are you protecting? _____

Again, ask: "How am I feeling toward this part, now?" _____.
Tell the part. Ask other parts to soften if they interfere with your Self-Energy, e.g. compassion.

Set your intentions: Listen to your deepest impulse, and be aware of how you would authentically like to feel, if you weren't under the influence of this part. Choose the Self-Energy quality, below, that matches how you *want* to be today, in contrast to what you noticed in Step Two. Circle it below and set your intention to cultivate and hold this quality today, being aware of and manager parts that try to take over. For example: "Today I want to feel my innate confidence. I open to my confidence as the core of my being." Write your intention: _____
_____

Calm   Curiosity   Connectedness   Clarity   Compassion   Courage   Confidence   Creativity

4. Negotiate/Ask: Repeat your intention silently to your parts. Then begin leading your system of parts, asking for their cooperation:

a). Negotiate this plan by first asking the parts if they notice you and how much you care. If so, ask if they would relax, trust you, and open space for you to be Present.

They do not need to force or make this happen. They can relax while you open.

b). Be aware of (and name) any parts that resist the plan, listen to their perspectives, and keep on negotiating with them.*

5. Open/Own It: When you feel a sense of permission, get centered again by focusing on the flow of your breath, relax, and bring your fullest attention to the present moment. Find stillness. Rest there. Allow calm to arise, first. Feel your Presence. Breathe and allow your chosen quality (or others) to emerge naturally. Feel it in your body. Envision yourself being this way throughout your day. Own it. Allow it to resonate as your true, essential nature.**

Notes: _____
_____

6. Remember/Reinforce: Create a plan to remember and cultivate your chosen Self-Energy quality for today. Set alarms or reminders on your phone, naming your quality, plan pleasant activities, be aware of obstacles presented by oppositional parts. My plan for today includes:
_____
_____

Evening Reflections: How did the day go? Was I aware? What parts got triggered? Did I bring compassion-appreciation to all parts? Are there any parts who still need my attention? If so, befriend them. Notes: _____

* If you have difficulty getting beyond this point, seek support from an IFS professional. The resistance is a healing opportunity, not a failure. Never push away a part. All parts are welcome.

** The recording; Meditations for Self-Awareness and Self-Leadership aligns with and supports this process. To order, go to www.holisticcounselwny.com, and download more SIT Sheets for free.

Additional Notes or Parts Mapping:

Self-Inquiry Tracking (SIT) Journal Sheet   Date _____

1. Center: Focus on the flow of your breathing. Don't clear away your thoughts. Just be aware…

2. Notice: What's on your mind? List prominent thoughts/emotions/sensations. Name the part.

Thoughts   ——>   Emotions   ——>   Bodily Sensations   ——>   Name of Part

Ask yourself: "How do I *feel toward* this part of me?" _____
"Can I be curious, compassionate or nonjudgmental?" _____
If so, go to Step Three. If not, you have another part blocking your Self-Energy. Be inquisitive about the interference. What's it about? _____.
After listening, kindly ask the interfering part to relax and allow you to be more open and present. If the resistance won't relax, do Step Three with the resistant part. If the resistance relaxes, you can continue, focusing on the part you originally noticed.

3. Listen: In a neutral, curious way, get to know the part of you identified in Step Two. Ask whatever questions you are curious about, such as:
   a). What is your purpose (or job) within my system? _____
   b). *How* do you do your job? _____
   c). How long have you been doing this, and what is it like for you to have this job? _____
   _____
   d). What are you afraid will happen if you stop doing your job? _____
   e). What are you protecting? _____

Again, ask: "How am I feeling toward this part, now?" _____.
Tell the part. Ask other parts to soften if they interfere with your Self-Energy, e.g. compassion.

Set your intentions: Listen to your deepest impulse, and be aware of how you would authentically like to feel, if you weren't under the influence of this part. Choose the Self-Energy quality, below, that matches how you *want* to be today, in contrast to what you noticed in Step Two. Circle it below and set your intention to cultivate and hold this quality today, being aware of and manager parts that try to take over. For example: "Today I want to feel my innate confidence. I open to my confidence as the core of my being." Write your intention: _____
_____

Calm   Curiosity   Connectedness   Clarity   Compassion   Courage   Confidence   Creativity

4. Negotiate/Ask: Repeat your intention silently to your parts. Then begin leading your system of parts, asking for their cooperation:

    a). Negotiate this plan by first asking the parts if they notice you and how much you care. If so, ask if they would relax, trust you, and open space for you to be Present.

        They do not need to force or make this happen. They can relax while you open.

    b). Be aware of (and name) any parts that resist the plan, listen to their perspectives, and keep on negotiating with them.*

5. Open/Own It: When you feel a sense of permission, get centered again by focusing on the flow of your breath, relax, and bring your fullest attention to the present moment. Find stillness. Rest there. Allow calm to arise, first. Feel your Presence. Breathe and allow your chosen quality (or others) to emerge naturally. Feel it in your body. Envision yourself being this way throughout your day. Own it. Allow it to resonate as your true, essential nature.**
Notes: _____
_____

6. Remember/Reinforce: Create a plan to remember and cultivate your chosen Self-Energy quality for today. Set alarms or reminders on your phone, naming your quality, plan pleasant activities, be aware of obstacles presented by oppositional parts. My plan for today includes:
_____
_____

Evening Reflections: How did the day go? Was I aware? What parts got triggered? Did I bring compassion-appreciation to all parts? Are there any parts who still need my attention? If so, befriend them. Notes: _____

* If you have difficulty getting beyond this point, seek support from an IFS professional. The resistance is a healing opportunity, not a failure. Never push away a part. All parts are welcome.

** The recording; Meditations for Self-Awareness and Self-Leadership aligns with and supports this process. To order, go to www.holisticcounselwny.com, and download more SIT Sheets for free.

Additional Notes or Parts Mapping:

Self-Inquiry Tracking (SIT) Journal Sheet   Date _____

1. Center: Focus on the flow of your breathing. Don't clear away your thoughts. Just be aware...

2. Notice: What's on your mind? List prominent thoughts/emotions/sensations. Name the part.

Thoughts ——> Emotions ——> Bodily Sensations ——> Name of Part

Ask yourself: "How do I *feel toward* this part of me?" _____
"Can I be curious, compassionate or nonjudgmental?" _____
If so, go to Step Three. If not, you have another part blocking your Self-Energy. Be inquisitive about the interference. What's it about? _____.
After listening, kindly ask the interfering part to relax and allow you to be more open and present. If the resistance won't relax, do Step Three with the resistant part. If the resistance relaxes, you can continue, focusing on the part you originally noticed.

3. Listen: In a neutral, curious way, get to know the part of you identified in Step Two. Ask whatever questions you are curious about, such as:
   a). What is your purpose (or job) within my system? _____
   b). *How* do you do your job? _____
   c). How long have you been doing this, and what is it like for you to have this job? _____
   _____
   d). What are you afraid will happen if you stop doing your job? _____
   e). What are you protecting? _____

Again, ask: "How am I feeling toward this part, now?" _____.
Tell the part. Ask other parts to soften if they interfere with your Self-Energy, e.g. compassion.

Set your intentions: Listen to your deepest impulse, and be aware of how you would authentically like to feel, if you weren't under the influence of this part. Choose the Self-Energy quality, below, that matches how you *want* to be today, in contrast to what you noticed in Step Two. Circle it below and set your intention to cultivate and hold this quality today, being aware of and manager parts that try to take over. For example: "Today I want to feel my innate confidence. I open to my confidence as the core of my being." Write your intention: _____
_____

Calm   Curiosity   Connectedness   Clarity   Compassion   Courage   Confidence   Creativity

4. Negotiate/Ask: Repeat your intention silently to your parts. Then begin leading your system of parts, asking for their cooperation:

a). Negotiate this plan by first asking the parts if they notice you and how much you care. If so, ask if they would relax, trust you, and open space for you to be Present.

They do not need to force or make this happen. They can relax while you open.

b). Be aware of (and name) any parts that resist the plan, listen to their perspectives, and keep on negotiating with them.*

5. Open/Own It: When you feel a sense of permission, get centered again by focusing on the flow of your breath, relax, and bring your fullest attention to the present moment. Find stillness. Rest there. Allow calm to arise, first. Feel your Presence. Breathe and allow your chosen quality (or others) to emerge naturally. Feel it in your body. Envision yourself being this way throughout your day. Own it. Allow it to resonate as your true, essential nature.**

Notes: _____

_____

6. Remember/Reinforce: Create a plan to remember and cultivate your chosen Self-Energy quality for today. Set alarms or reminders on your phone, naming your quality, plan pleasant activities, be aware of obstacles presented by oppositional parts. My plan for today includes:

_____

_____

Evening Reflections: How did the day go? Was I aware? What parts got triggered? Did I bring compassion-appreciation to all parts? Are there any parts who still need my attention? If so, befriend them. Notes: _____

* If you have difficulty getting beyond this point, seek support from an IFS professional. The resistance is a healing opportunity, not a failure. Never push away a part. All parts are welcome.

** The recording; Meditations for Self-Awareness and Self-Leadership aligns with and supports this process. To order, go to www.holisticcounselwny.com, and download more SIT Sheets for free.

Additional Notes or Parts Mapping:

Self-Inquiry Tracking (SIT) Journal Sheet   Date _____

1. Center: Focus on the flow of your breathing. Don't clear away your thoughts. Just be aware...

2. Notice: What's on your mind? List prominent thoughts/emotions/sensations. Name the part.

Thoughts ——> Emotions ——> Bodily Sensations ——> Name of Part

Ask yourself: "How do I *feel toward* this part of me?" _____
"Can I be curious, compassionate or nonjudgmental?" _____
If so, go to Step Three. If not, you have another part blocking your Self-Energy. Be inquisitive about the interference. What's it about? _____.
After listening, kindly ask the interfering part to relax and allow you to be more open and present. If the resistance won't relax, do Step Three with the resistant part. If the resistance relaxes, you can continue, focusing on the part you originally noticed.

3. Listen: In a neutral, curious way, get to know the part of you identified in Step Two. Ask whatever questions you are curious about, such as:
   a). What is your purpose (or job) within my system? _____
   b). *How* do you do your job? _____
   c). How long have you been doing this, and what is it like for you to have this job? _____
   _____
   d). What are you afraid will happen if you stop doing your job? _____
   e). What are you protecting? _____

Again, ask: "How am I feeling toward this part, now?" _____.
Tell the part. Ask other parts to soften if they interfere with your Self-Energy, e.g. compassion.

Set your intentions: Listen to your deepest impulse, and be aware of how you would authentically like to feel, if you weren't under the influence of this part. Choose the Self-Energy quality, below, that matches how you *want* to be today, in contrast to what you noticed in Step Two. Circle it below and set your intention to cultivate and hold this quality today, being aware of and manager parts that try to take over. For example: "Today I want to feel my innate confidence. I open to my confidence as the core of my being." Write your intention: _____
_____

Calm   Curiosity   Connectedness   Clarity   Compassion   Courage   Confidence   Creativity

4. Negotiate/Ask: Repeat your intention silently to your parts. Then begin leading your system of parts, asking for their cooperation:

    a). Negotiate this plan by first asking the parts if they notice you and how much you care. If so, ask if they would relax, trust you, and open space for you to be Present.

        They do not need to force or make this happen. They can relax while you open.

    b). Be aware of (and name) any parts that resist the plan, listen to their perspectives, and keep on negotiating with them.*

5. Open/Own It: When you feel a sense of permission, get centered again by focusing on the flow of your breath, relax, and bring your fullest attention to the present moment. Find stillness. Rest there. Allow calm to arise, first. Feel your Presence. Breathe and allow your chosen quality (or others) to emerge naturally. Feel it in your body. Envision yourself being this way throughout your day. Own it. Allow it to resonate as your true, essential nature.**

Notes: _____

_____

6. Remember/Reinforce: Create a plan to remember and cultivate your chosen Self-Energy quality for today. Set alarms or reminders on your phone, naming your quality, plan pleasant activities, be aware of obstacles presented by oppositional parts. My plan for today includes:

_____

_____

Evening Reflections: How did the day go? Was I aware? What parts got triggered? Did I bring compassion-appreciation to all parts? Are there any parts who still need my attention? If so, befriend them. Notes: _____

* If you have difficulty getting beyond this point, seek support from an IFS professional. The resistance is a healing opportunity, not a failure. Never push away a part. All parts are welcome.

** The recording; Meditations for Self-Awareness and Self-Leadership aligns with and supports this process. To order, go to www.holisticcounselwny.com, and download more SIT Sheets for free.

Additional Notes or Parts Mapping:

Self-Inquiry Tracking (SIT) Journal Sheet   Date _____

1. Center: Focus on the flow of your breathing. Don't clear away your thoughts. Just be aware...

2. Notice: What's on your mind? List prominent thoughts/emotions/sensations. Name the part.

Thoughts   ——>   Emotions   ——>   Bodily Sensations   ——>   Name of Part

Ask yourself: "How do I *feel toward* this part of me?" _____
"Can I be curious, compassionate or nonjudgmental?" _____
If so, go to Step Three. If not, you have another part blocking your Self-Energy. Be inquisitive about the interference. What's it about? _____.
After listening, kindly ask the interfering part to relax and allow you to be more open and present. If the resistance won't relax, do Step Three with the resistant part. If the resistance relaxes, you can continue, focusing on the part you originally noticed.

3. Listen: In a neutral, curious way, get to know the part of you identified in Step Two. Ask whatever questions you are curious about, such as:
 a). What is your purpose (or job) within my system? _____
 b). *How* do you do your job? _____
 c). How long have you been doing this, and what is it like for you to have this job? _____
 _____
 d). What are you afraid will happen if you stop doing your job? _____
 e). What are you protecting? _____

Again, ask: "How am I feeling toward this part, now?" _____.
Tell the part. Ask other parts to soften if they interfere with your Self-Energy, e.g. compassion.

Set your intentions: Listen to your deepest impulse, and be aware of how you would authentically like to feel, if you weren't under the influence of this part. Choose the Self-Energy quality, below, that matches how you *want* to be today, in contrast to what you noticed in Step Two. Circle it below and set your intention to cultivate and hold this quality today, being aware of and manager parts that try to take over. For example: "Today I want to feel my innate confidence. I open to my confidence as the core of my being." Write your intention: _____
_____

Calm   Curiosity   Connectedness   Clarity   Compassion   Courage   Confidence   Creativity

4. Negotiate/Ask: Repeat your intention silently to your parts. Then begin leading your system of parts, asking for their cooperation:

   a). Negotiate this plan by first asking the parts if they notice you and how much you care. If so, ask if they would relax, trust you, and open space for you to be Present.

   They do not need to force or make this happen. They can relax while you open.

   b). Be aware of (and name) any parts that resist the plan, listen to their perspectives, and keep on negotiating with them.*

5. Open/Own It: When you feel a sense of permission, get centered again by focusing on the flow of your breath, relax, and bring your fullest attention to the present moment. Find stillness. Rest there. Allow calm to arise, first. Feel your Presence. Breathe and allow your chosen quality (or others) to emerge naturally. Feel it in your body. Envision yourself being this way throughout your day. Own it. Allow it to resonate as your true, essential nature.**
Notes: _____
_____

6. Remember/Reinforce: Create a plan to remember and cultivate your chosen Self-Energy quality for today. Set alarms or reminders on your phone, naming your quality, plan pleasant activities, be aware of obstacles presented by oppositional parts. My plan for today includes:
_____
_____

Evening Reflections: How did the day go? Was I aware? What parts got triggered? Did I bring compassion-appreciation to all parts? Are there any parts who still need my attention? If so, befriend them. Notes: _____

* If you have difficulty getting beyond this point, seek support from an IFS professional. The resistance is a healing opportunity, not a failure. Never push away a part. All parts are welcome.

** The recording; Meditations for Self-Awareness and Self-Leadership aligns with and supports this process. To order, go to www.holisticcounselwny.com, and download more SIT Sheets for free.

Additional Notes or Parts Mapping:

Self-Inquiry Tracking (SIT) Journal Sheet   Date _____

1. Center: Focus on the flow of your breathing. Don't clear away your thoughts. Just be aware…

2. Notice: What's on your mind? List prominent thoughts/emotions/sensations. Name the part.

Thoughts   ——>   Emotions   ——>   Bodily Sensations   ——>   Name of Part

Ask yourself: "How do I *feel toward* this part of me?" _____
"Can I be curious, compassionate or nonjudgmental?" _____
If so, go to Step Three. If not, you have another part blocking your Self-Energy. Be inquisitive about the interference. What's it about? _____.
After listening, kindly ask the interfering part to relax and allow you to be more open and present. If the resistance won't relax, do Step Three with the resistant part. If the resistance relaxes, you can continue, focusing on the part you originally noticed.

3. Listen: In a neutral, curious way, get to know the part of you identified in Step Two. Ask whatever questions you are curious about, such as:

  a). What is your purpose (or job) within my system? _____
  b). *How* do you do your job? _____
  c). How long have you been doing this, and what is it like for you to have this job? _____
  _____
  d). What are you afraid will happen if you stop doing your job? _____
  e). What are you protecting? _____

Again, ask: "How am I feeling toward this part, now?" _____.
Tell the part. Ask other parts to soften if they interfere with your Self-Energy, e.g. compassion.

Set your intentions: Listen to your deepest impulse, and be aware of how you would authentically like to feel, if you weren't under the influence of this part. Choose the Self-Energy quality, below, that matches how you *want* to be today, in contrast to what you noticed in Step Two. Circle it below and set your intention to cultivate and hold this quality today, being aware of and manager parts that try to take over. For example: "Today I want to feel my innate confidence. I open to my confidence as the core of my being." Write your intention: _____
_____

Calm   Curiosity   Connectedness   Clarity   Compassion   Courage   Confidence   Creativity

4. Negotiate/Ask: Repeat your intention silently to your parts. Then begin leading your system of parts, asking for their cooperation:

    a). Negotiate this plan by first asking the parts if they notice you and how much you care. If so, ask if they would relax, trust you, and open space for you to be Present.

        They do not need to force or make this happen. They can relax while you open.

    b). Be aware of (and name) any parts that resist the plan, listen to their perspectives, and keep on negotiating with them.*

5. Open/Own It: When you feel a sense of permission, get centered again by focusing on the flow of your breath, relax, and bring your fullest attention to the present moment. Find stillness. Rest there. Allow calm to arise, first. Feel your Presence. Breathe and allow your chosen quality (or others) to emerge naturally. Feel it in your body. Envision yourself being this way throughout your day. Own it. Allow it to resonate as your true, essential nature.**

Notes: _____

_____

6. Remember/Reinforce: Create a plan to remember and cultivate your chosen Self-Energy quality for today. Set alarms or reminders on your phone, naming your quality, plan pleasant activities, be aware of obstacles presented by oppositional parts. My plan for today includes:

_____

_____

Evening Reflections: How did the day go? Was I aware? What parts got triggered? Did I bring compassion-appreciation to all parts? Are there any parts who still need my attention? If so, befriend them. Notes: _____

* If you have difficulty getting beyond this point, seek support from an IFS professional. The resistance is a healing opportunity, not a failure. Never push away a part. All parts are welcome.

** The recording; Meditations for Self-Awareness and Self-Leadership aligns with and supports this process. To order, go to www.holisticcounselwny.com, and download more SIT Sheets for free.

Additional Notes or Parts Mapping:

Self-Inquiry Tracking (SIT) Journal Sheet   Date _____

1. Center: Focus on the flow of your breathing. Don't clear away your thoughts. Just be aware…

2. Notice: What's on your mind? List prominent thoughts/emotions/sensations. Name the part.

Thoughts ——> Emotions ——> Bodily Sensations ——> Name of Part

Ask yourself: "How do I *feel toward* this part of me?" _____
"Can I be curious, compassionate or nonjudgmental?" _____
If so, go to Step Three. If not, you have another part blocking your Self-Energy. Be inquisitive about the interference. What's it about? _____.
After listening, kindly ask the interfering part to relax and allow you to be more open and present. If the resistance won't relax, do Step Three with the resistant part. If the resistance relaxes, you can continue, focusing on the part you originally noticed.

3. Listen: In a neutral, curious way, get to know the part of you identified in Step Two. Ask whatever questions you are curious about, such as:

   a). What is your purpose (or job) within my system? _____
   b). *How* do you do your job? _____
   c). How long have you been doing this, and what is it like for you to have this job? _____
   _____
   d). What are you afraid will happen if you stop doing your job? _____
   e). What are you protecting? _____

Again, ask: "How am I feeling toward this part, now?" _____.
Tell the part. Ask other parts to soften if they interfere with your Self-Energy, e.g. compassion.

Set your intentions: Listen to your deepest impulse, and be aware of how you would authentically like to feel, if you weren't under the influence of this part. Choose the Self-Energy quality, below, that matches how you *want* to be today, in contrast to what you noticed in Step Two. Circle it below and set your intention to cultivate and hold this quality today, being aware of and manager parts that try to take over. For example: "Today I want to feel my innate confidence. I open to my confidence as the core of my being." Write your intention: _____
_____

Calm   Curiosity   Connectedness   Clarity   Compassion   Courage   Confidence   Creativity

4. Negotiate/Ask: Repeat your intention silently to your parts. Then begin leading your system of parts, asking for their cooperation:

a). Negotiate this plan by first asking the parts if they notice you and how much you care. If so, ask if they would relax, trust you, and open space for you to be Present.

They do not need to force or make this happen. They can relax while you open.

b). Be aware of (and name) any parts that resist the plan, listen to their perspectives, and keep on negotiating with them.*

5. Open/Own It: When you feel a sense of permission, get centered again by focusing on the flow of your breath, relax, and bring your fullest attention to the present moment. Find stillness. Rest there. Allow calm to arise, first. Feel your Presence. Breathe and allow your chosen quality (or others) to emerge naturally. Feel it in your body. Envision yourself being this way throughout your day. Own it. Allow it to resonate as your true, essential nature.**

Notes: _____

_____

6. Remember/Reinforce: Create a plan to remember and cultivate your chosen Self-Energy quality for today. Set alarms or reminders on your phone, naming your quality, plan pleasant activities, be aware of obstacles presented by oppositional parts. My plan for today includes:

_____

_____

Evening Reflections: How did the day go? Was I aware? What parts got triggered? Did I bring compassion-appreciation to all parts? Are there any parts who still need my attention? If so, befriend them. Notes: _____

* If you have difficulty getting beyond this point, seek support from an IFS professional. The resistance is a healing opportunity, not a failure. Never push away a part. All parts are welcome.

** The recording; Meditations for Self-Awareness and Self-Leadership aligns with and supports this process. To order, go to www.holisticcounselwny.com, and download more SIT Sheets for free.

Additional Notes or Parts Mapping:

Self-Inquiry Tracking (SIT) Journal Sheet   Date _____

1. Center: Focus on the flow of your breathing. Don't clear away your thoughts. Just be aware...

2. Notice: What's on your mind? List prominent thoughts/emotions/sensations. Name the part.

Thoughts ——> Emotions ——> Bodily Sensations ——> Name of Part

Ask yourself: "How do I *feel toward* this part of me?" _____
"Can I be curious, compassionate or nonjudgmental?" _____
If so, go to Step Three. If not, you have another part blocking your Self-Energy. Be inquisitive about the interference. What's it about? _____.
After listening, kindly ask the interfering part to relax and allow you to be more open and present. If the resistance won't relax, do Step Three with the resistant part. If the resistance relaxes, you can continue, focusing on the part you originally noticed.

3. Listen: In a neutral, curious way, get to know the part of you identified in Step Two. Ask whatever questions you are curious about, such as:
   a). What is your purpose (or job) within my system? _____
   b). *How* do you do your job? _____
   c). How long have you been doing this, and what is it like for you to have this job? _____
   _____
   d). What are you afraid will happen if you stop doing your job? _____
   e). What are you protecting? _____

Again, ask: "How am I feeling toward this part, now?" _____.
Tell the part. Ask other parts to soften if they interfere with your Self-Energy, e.g. compassion.

Set your intentions: Listen to your deepest impulse, and be aware of how you would authentically like to feel, if you weren't under the influence of this part. Choose the Self-Energy quality, below, that matches how you *want* to be today, in contrast to what you noticed in Step Two. Circle it below and set your intention to cultivate and hold this quality today, being aware of and manager parts that try to take over. For example: "Today I want to feel my innate confidence. I open to my confidence as the core of my being." Write your intention: _____
_____

Calm   Curiosity   Connectedness   Clarity   Compassion   Courage   Confidence   Creativity

4. Negotiate/Ask: Repeat your intention silently to your parts. Then begin leading your system of parts, asking for their cooperation:

    a). Negotiate this plan by first asking the parts if they notice you and how much you care. If so, ask if they would relax, trust you, and open space for you to be Present.

        They do not need to force or make this happen. They can relax while you open.

    b). Be aware of (and name) any parts that resist the plan, listen to their perspectives, and keep on negotiating with them.*

5. Open/Own It: When you feel a sense of permission, get centered again by focusing on the flow of your breath, relax, and bring your fullest attention to the present moment. Find stillness. Rest there. Allow calm to arise, first. Feel your Presence. Breathe and allow your chosen quality (or others) to emerge naturally. Feel it in your body. Envision yourself being this way throughout your day. Own it. Allow it to resonate as your true, essential nature.**

Notes: _____

_____

6. Remember/Reinforce: Create a plan to remember and cultivate your chosen Self-Energy quality for today. Set alarms or reminders on your phone, naming your quality, plan pleasant activities, be aware of obstacles presented by oppositional parts. My plan for today includes:

_____

_____

Evening Reflections: How did the day go? Was I aware? What parts got triggered? Did I bring compassion-appreciation to all parts? Are there any parts who still need my attention? If so, befriend them. Notes: _____

* If you have difficulty getting beyond this point, seek support from an IFS professional. The resistance is a healing opportunity, not a failure. Never push away a part. All parts are welcome.

** The recording; Meditations for Self-Awareness and Self-Leadership aligns with and supports this process. To order, go to www.holisticcounselwny.com, and download more SIT Sheets for free.

Additional Notes or Parts Mapping:

Self-Inquiry Tracking (SIT) Journal Sheet   Date _____

1. Center: Focus on the flow of your breathing. Don't clear away your thoughts. Just be aware…

2. Notice: What's on your mind? List prominent thoughts/emotions/sensations. Name the part.

Thoughts ——> Emotions ——> Bodily Sensations ——> Name of Part

Ask yourself: "How do I *feel toward* this part of me?" _____
"Can I be curious, compassionate or nonjudgmental?" _____
If so, go to Step Three. If not, you have another part blocking your Self-Energy. Be inquisitive about the interference. What's it about? _____.
After listening, kindly ask the interfering part to relax and allow you to be more open and present. If the resistance won't relax, do Step Three with the resistant part. If the resistance relaxes, you can continue, focusing on the part you originally noticed.

3. Listen: In a neutral, curious way, get to know the part of you identified in Step Two. Ask whatever questions you are curious about, such as:

    a). What is your purpose (or job) within my system? _____
    b). *How* do you do your job? _____
    c). How long have you been doing this, and what is it like for you to have this job? _____
    _____
    d). What are you afraid will happen if you stop doing your job? _____
    e). What are you protecting? _____

Again, ask: "How am I feeling toward this part, now?" _____.
Tell the part. Ask other parts to soften if they interfere with your Self-Energy, e.g. compassion.

Set your intentions: Listen to your deepest impulse, and be aware of how you would authentically like to feel, if you weren't under the influence of this part. Choose the Self-Energy quality, below, that matches how you *want* to be today, in contrast to what you noticed in Step Two. Circle it below and set your intention to cultivate and hold this quality today, being aware of and manager parts that try to take over. For example: "Today I want to feel my innate confidence. I open to my confidence as the core of my being." Write your intention: _____
_____

Calm   Curiosity   Connectedness   Clarity   Compassion   Courage   Confidence   Creativity

4. Negotiate/Ask: Repeat your intention silently to your parts. Then begin leading your system of parts, asking for their cooperation:

a). Negotiate this plan by first asking the parts if they notice you and how much you care. If so, ask if they would relax, trust you, and open space for you to be Present.

They do not need to force or make this happen. They can relax while you open.

b). Be aware of (and name) any parts that resist the plan, listen to their perspectives, and keep on negotiating with them.*

5. Open/Own It: When you feel a sense of permission, get centered again by focusing on the flow of your breath, relax, and bring your fullest attention to the present moment. Find stillness. Rest there. Allow calm to arise, first. Feel your Presence. Breathe and allow your chosen quality (or others) to emerge naturally. Feel it in your body. Envision yourself being this way throughout your day. Own it. Allow it to resonate as your true, essential nature.**
Notes: _____
_____

6. Remember/Reinforce: Create a plan to remember and cultivate your chosen Self-Energy quality for today. Set alarms or reminders on your phone, naming your quality, plan pleasant activities, be aware of obstacles presented by oppositional parts. My plan for today includes:
_____
_____

Evening Reflections: How did the day go? Was I aware? What parts got triggered? Did I bring compassion-appreciation to all parts? Are there any parts who still need my attention? If so, befriend them. Notes: _____

* If you have difficulty getting beyond this point, seek support from an IFS professional. The resistance is a healing opportunity, not a failure. Never push away a part. All parts are welcome.

** The recording; Meditations for Self-Awareness and Self-Leadership aligns with and supports this process. To order, go to www.holisticcounselwny.com, and download more SIT Sheets for free.

Additional Notes or Parts Mapping:

Self-Inquiry Tracking (SIT) Journal Sheet   Date _____

1. Center: Focus on the flow of your breathing. Don't clear away your thoughts. Just be aware...

2. Notice: What's on your mind? List prominent thoughts/emotions/sensations. Name the part.

Thoughts ——> Emotions ——> Bodily Sensations ——> Name of Part

Ask yourself: "How do I *feel toward* this part of me?" _____
"Can I be curious, compassionate or nonjudgmental?" _____
If so, go to Step Three. If not, you have another part blocking your Self-Energy. Be inquisitive about the interference. What's it about? _____.
After listening, kindly ask the interfering part to relax and allow you to be more open and present. If the resistance won't relax, do Step Three with the resistant part. If the resistance relaxes, you can continue, focusing on the part you originally noticed.

3. Listen: In a neutral, curious way, get to know the part of you identified in Step Two. Ask whatever questions you are curious about, such as:

    a). What is your purpose (or job) within my system? _____
    b). *How* do you do your job? _____
    c). How long have you been doing this, and what is it like for you to have this job? _____
    _____
    d). What are you afraid will happen if you stop doing your job? _____
    e). What are you protecting? _____

Again, ask: "How am I feeling toward this part, now?" _____.
Tell the part. Ask other parts to soften if they interfere with your Self-Energy, e.g. compassion.

Set your intentions: Listen to your deepest impulse, and be aware of how you would authentically like to feel, if you weren't under the influence of this part. Choose the Self-Energy quality, below, that matches how you *want* to be today, in contrast to what you noticed in Step Two. Circle it below and set your intention to cultivate and hold this quality today, being aware of and manager parts that try to take over. For example: "Today I want to feel my innate confidence. I open to my confidence as the core of my being." Write your intention: _____
_____

Calm   Curiosity   Connectedness   Clarity   Compassion   Courage   Confidence   Creativity

4. Negotiate/Ask: Repeat your intention silently to your parts. Then begin leading your system of parts, asking for their cooperation:

    a). Negotiate this plan by first asking the parts if they notice you and how much you care. If so, ask if they would relax, trust you, and open space for you to be Present.

        They do not need to force or make this happen. They can relax while you open.

    b). Be aware of (and name) any parts that resist the plan, listen to their perspectives, and keep on negotiating with them.*

5. Open/Own It: When you feel a sense of permission, get centered again by focusing on the flow of your breath, relax, and bring your fullest attention to the present moment. Find stillness. Rest there. Allow calm to arise, first. Feel your Presence. Breathe and allow your chosen quality (or others) to emerge naturally. Feel it in your body. Envision yourself being this way throughout your day. Own it. Allow it to resonate as your true, essential nature.**
Notes: _____
_____

6. Remember/Reinforce: Create a plan to remember and cultivate your chosen Self-Energy quality for today. Set alarms or reminders on your phone, naming your quality, plan pleasant activities, be aware of obstacles presented by oppositional parts. My plan for today includes:
_____
_____

Evening Reflections: How did the day go? Was I aware? What parts got triggered? Did I bring compassion-appreciation to all parts? Are there any parts who still need my attention? If so, befriend them. Notes: _____

* If you have difficulty getting beyond this point, seek support from an IFS professional. The resistance is a healing opportunity, not a failure. Never push away a part. All parts are welcome.

** The recording; Meditations for Self-Awareness and Self-Leadership aligns with and supports this process. To order, go to www.holisticcounselwny.com, and download more SIT Sheets for free.

Additional Notes or Parts Mapping:

Self-Inquiry Tracking (SIT) Journal Sheet   Date _____

1. Center: Focus on the flow of your breathing. Don't clear away your thoughts. Just be aware...

2. Notice: What's on your mind? List prominent thoughts/emotions/sensations. Name the part.

Thoughts ——> Emotions ——> Bodily Sensations ——> Name of Part

Ask yourself: "How do I *feel toward* this part of me?" _____
"Can I be curious, compassionate or nonjudgmental?" _____
If so, go to Step Three. If not, you have another part blocking your Self-Energy. Be inquisitive about the interference. What's it about? _____.
After listening, kindly ask the interfering part to relax and allow you to be more open and present. If the resistance won't relax, do Step Three with the resistant part. If the resistance relaxes, you can continue, focusing on the part you originally noticed.

3. Listen: In a neutral, curious way, get to know the part of you identified in Step Two. Ask whatever questions you are curious about, such as:

    a). What is your purpose (or job) within my system? _____
    b). *How* do you do your job? _____
    c). How long have you been doing this, and what is it like for you to have this job? _____
    _____
    d). What are you afraid will happen if you stop doing your job? _____
    e). What are you protecting? _____

Again, ask: "How am I feeling toward this part, now?" _____.
Tell the part. Ask other parts to soften if they interfere with your Self-Energy, e.g. compassion.

Set your intentions: Listen to your deepest impulse, and be aware of how you would authentically like to feel, if you weren't under the influence of this part. Choose the Self-Energy quality, below, that matches how you *want* to be today, in contrast to what you noticed in Step Two. Circle it below and set your intention to cultivate and hold this quality today, being aware of and manager parts that try to take over. For example: "Today I want to feel my innate confidence. I open to my confidence as the core of my being." Write your intention: _____
_____

Calm   Curiosity   Connectedness   Clarity   Compassion   Courage   Confidence   Creativity

4. Negotiate/Ask: Repeat your intention silently to your parts. Then begin leading your system of parts, asking for their cooperation:

a). Negotiate this plan by first asking the parts if they notice you and how much you care. If so, ask if they would relax, trust you, and open space for you to be Present.

They do not need to force or make this happen. They can relax while you open.

b). Be aware of (and name) any parts that resist the plan, listen to their perspectives, and keep on negotiating with them.*

5. Open/Own It: When you feel a sense of permission, get centered again by focusing on the flow of your breath, relax, and bring your fullest attention to the present moment. Find stillness. Rest there. Allow calm to arise, first. Feel your Presence. Breathe and allow your chosen quality (or others) to emerge naturally. Feel it in your body. Envision yourself being this way throughout your day. Own it. Allow it to resonate as your true, essential nature.**
Notes: _____
_____

6. Remember/Reinforce: Create a plan to remember and cultivate your chosen Self-Energy quality for today. Set alarms or reminders on your phone, naming your quality, plan pleasant activities, be aware of obstacles presented by oppositional parts. My plan for today includes:
_____
_____

Evening Reflections: How did the day go? Was I aware? What parts got triggered? Did I bring compassion-appreciation to all parts? Are there any parts who still need my attention? If so, befriend them. Notes: _____

* If you have difficulty getting beyond this point, seek support from an IFS professional. The resistance is a healing opportunity, not a failure. Never push away a part. All parts are welcome.

** The recording; Meditations for Self-Awareness and Self-Leadership aligns with and supports this process. To order, go to www.holisticcounselwny.com, and download more SIT Sheets for free.

Additional Notes or Parts Mapping:

Self-Inquiry Tracking (SIT) Journal Sheet   Date _____

1. Center: Focus on the flow of your breathing. Don't clear away your thoughts. Just be aware…

2. Notice: What's on your mind? List prominent thoughts/emotions/sensations. Name the part.

Thoughts   ——>   Emotions   ——>   Bodily Sensations   ——>   Name of Part

Ask yourself: "How do I *feel toward* this part of me?" _____
"Can I be curious, compassionate or nonjudgmental?" _____
If so, go to Step Three. If not, you have another part blocking your Self-Energy. Be inquisitive about the interference. What's it about? _____.
After listening, kindly ask the interfering part to relax and allow you to be more open and present. If the resistance won't relax, do Step Three with the resistant part. If the resistance relaxes, you can continue, focusing on the part you originally noticed.

3. Listen: In a neutral, curious way, get to know the part of you identified in Step Two. Ask whatever questions you are curious about, such as:

    a). What is your purpose (or job) within my system? _____
    b). *How* do you do your job? _____
    c). How long have you been doing this, and what is it like for you to have this job? _____

    d). What are you afraid will happen if you stop doing your job? _____
    e). What are you protecting? _____

Again, ask: "How am I feeling toward this part, now?" _____.
Tell the part. Ask other parts to soften if they interfere with your Self-Energy, e.g. compassion.

Set your intentions: Listen to your deepest impulse, and be aware of how you would authentically like to feel, if you weren't under the influence of this part. Choose the Self-Energy quality, below, that matches how you *want* to be today, in contrast to what you noticed in Step Two. Circle it below and set your intention to cultivate and hold this quality today, being aware of and manager parts that try to take over. For example: "Today I want to feel my innate confidence. I open to my confidence as the core of my being." Write your intention: _____
_____

Calm   Curiosity   Connectedness   Clarity   Compassion   Courage   Confidence   Creativity

4. Negotiate/Ask: Repeat your intention silently to your parts. Then begin leading your system of parts, asking for their cooperation:

    a). Negotiate this plan by first asking the parts if they notice you and how much you care. If so, ask if they would relax, trust you, and open space for you to be Present.

        They do not need to force or make this happen. They can relax while you open.

    b). Be aware of (and name) any parts that resist the plan, listen to their perspectives, and keep on negotiating with them.*

5. Open/Own It: When you feel a sense of permission, get centered again by focusing on the flow of your breath, relax, and bring your fullest attention to the present moment. Find stillness. Rest there. Allow calm to arise, first. Feel your Presence. Breathe and allow your chosen quality (or others) to emerge naturally. Feel it in your body. Envision yourself being this way throughout your day. Own it. Allow it to resonate as your true, essential nature.**

Notes: _____

_____

6. Remember/Reinforce: Create a plan to remember and cultivate your chosen Self-Energy quality for today. Set alarms or reminders on your phone, naming your quality, plan pleasant activities, be aware of obstacles presented by oppositional parts. My plan for today includes:

_____

_____

Evening Reflections: How did the day go? Was I aware? What parts got triggered? Did I bring compassion-appreciation to all parts? Are there any parts who still need my attention? If so, befriend them. Notes: _____

* If you have difficulty getting beyond this point, seek support from an IFS professional. The resistance is a healing opportunity, not a failure. Never push away a part. All parts are welcome.

** The recording; Meditations for Self-Awareness and Self-Leadership aligns with and supports this process. To order, go to www.holisticcounselwny.com, and download more SIT Sheets for free.

Additional Notes or Parts Mapping:

Self-Inquiry Tracking (SIT) Journal Sheet   Date _____

1. Center: Focus on the flow of your breathing. Don't clear away your thoughts. Just be aware...

2. Notice: What's on your mind? List prominent thoughts/emotions/sensations. Name the part.

Thoughts ——> Emotions ——> Bodily Sensations ——> Name of Part

Ask yourself: "How do I *feel toward* this part of me?" _____

"Can I be curious, compassionate or nonjudgmental?" _____

If so, go to Step Three. If not, you have another part blocking your Self-Energy. Be inquisitive about the interference. What's it about? _____.

After listening, kindly ask the interfering part to relax and allow you to be more open and present. If the resistance won't relax, do Step Three with the resistant part. If the resistance relaxes, you can continue, focusing on the part you originally noticed.

3. Listen: In a neutral, curious way, get to know the part of you identified in Step Two. Ask whatever questions you are curious about, such as:

    a). What is your purpose (or job) within my system? _____
    b). *How* do you do your job? _____
    c). How long have you been doing this, and what is it like for you to have this job? _____
    d). What are you afraid will happen if you stop doing your job? _____
    e). What are you protecting? _____

Again, ask: "How am I feeling toward this part, now?" _____.
Tell the part. Ask other parts to soften if they interfere with your Self-Energy, e.g. compassion.

Set your intentions: Listen to your deepest impulse, and be aware of how you would authentically like to feel, if you weren't under the influence of this part. Choose the Self-Energy quality, below, that matches how you *want* to be today, in contrast to what you noticed in Step Two. Circle it below and set your intention to cultivate and hold this quality today, being aware of and manager parts that try to take over. For example: "Today I want to feel my innate confidence. I open to my confidence as the core of my being." Write your intention: _____
_____

Calm   Curiosity   Connectedness   Clarity   Compassion   Courage   Confidence   Creativity

4. Negotiate/Ask: Repeat your intention silently to your parts. Then begin leading your system of parts, asking for their cooperation:

a). Negotiate this plan by first asking the parts if they notice you and how much you care. If so, ask if they would relax, trust you, and open space for you to be Present.

They do not need to force or make this happen. They can relax while you open.

b). Be aware of (and name) any parts that resist the plan, listen to their perspectives, and keep on negotiating with them.*

5. Open/Own It: When you feel a sense of permission, get centered again by focusing on the flow of your breath, relax, and bring your fullest attention to the present moment. Find stillness. Rest there. Allow calm to arise, first. Feel your Presence. Breathe and allow your chosen quality (or others) to emerge naturally. Feel it in your body. Envision yourself being this way throughout your day. Own it. Allow it to resonate as your true, essential nature.**
Notes: _____
_____

6. Remember/Reinforce: Create a plan to remember and cultivate your chosen Self-Energy quality for today. Set alarms or reminders on your phone, naming your quality, plan pleasant activities, be aware of obstacles presented by oppositional parts. My plan for today includes:
_____
_____

Evening Reflections: How did the day go? Was I aware? What parts got triggered? Did I bring compassion-appreciation to all parts? Are there any parts who still need my attention? If so, befriend them. Notes: _____

* If you have difficulty getting beyond this point, seek support from an IFS professional. The resistance is a healing opportunity, not a failure. Never push away a part. All parts are welcome.

** The recording; Meditations for Self-Awareness and Self-Leadership aligns with and supports this process. To order, go to www.holisticcounselwny.com, and download more SIT Sheets for free.

Additional Notes or Parts Mapping:

Self-Inquiry Tracking (SIT) Journal Sheet   Date _____

1. Center: Focus on the flow of your breathing. Don't clear away your thoughts. Just be aware…

2. Notice: What's on your mind? List prominent thoughts/emotions/sensations. Name the part.

Thoughts ——> Emotions ——> Bodily Sensations ——> Name of Part

Ask yourself: "How do I *feel toward* this part of me?" _____
"Can I be curious, compassionate or nonjudgmental?" _____
If so, go to Step Three. If not, you have another part blocking your Self-Energy. Be inquisitive about the interference. What's it about? _____.
After listening, kindly ask the interfering part to relax and allow you to be more open and present. If the resistance won't relax, do Step Three with the resistant part. If the resistance relaxes, you can continue, focusing on the part you originally noticed.

3. Listen: In a neutral, curious way, get to know the part of you identified in Step Two. Ask whatever questions you are curious about, such as:
   a). What is your purpose (or job) within my system? _____
   b). *How* do you do your job? _____
   c). How long have you been doing this, and what is it like for you to have this job? _____
   _____
   d). What are you afraid will happen if you stop doing your job? _____
   e). What are you protecting? _____

Again, ask: "How am I feeling toward this part, now?" _____.
Tell the part. Ask other parts to soften if they interfere with your Self-Energy, e.g. compassion.

Set your intentions: Listen to your deepest impulse, and be aware of how you would authentically like to feel, if you weren't under the influence of this part. Choose the Self-Energy quality, below, that matches how you *want* to be today, in contrast to what you noticed in Step Two. Circle it below and set your intention to cultivate and hold this quality today, being aware of and manager parts that try to take over. For example: "Today I want to feel my innate confidence. I open to my confidence as the core of my being." Write your intention: _____
_____

Calm   Curiosity   Connectedness   Clarity   Compassion   Courage   Confidence   Creativity

4. Negotiate/Ask: Repeat your intention silently to your parts. Then begin leading your system of parts, asking for their cooperation:

    a). Negotiate this plan by first asking the parts if they notice you and how much you care. If so, ask if they would relax, trust you, and open space for you to be Present.

        They do not need to force or make this happen. They can relax while you open.

    b). Be aware of (and name) any parts that resist the plan, listen to their perspectives, and keep on negotiating with them.*

5. Open/Own It: When you feel a sense of permission, get centered again by focusing on the flow of your breath, relax, and bring your fullest attention to the present moment. Find stillness. Rest there. Allow calm to arise, first. Feel your Presence. Breathe and allow your chosen quality (or others) to emerge naturally. Feel it in your body. Envision yourself being this way throughout your day. Own it. Allow it to resonate as your true, essential nature.**
Notes: _____
_____

6. Remember/Reinforce: Create a plan to remember and cultivate your chosen Self-Energy quality for today. Set alarms or reminders on your phone, naming your quality, plan pleasant activities, be aware of obstacles presented by oppositional parts. My plan for today includes:
_____
_____

Evening Reflections: How did the day go? Was I aware? What parts got triggered? Did I bring compassion-appreciation to all parts? Are there any parts who still need my attention? If so, befriend them. Notes: _____

* If you have difficulty getting beyond this point, seek support from an IFS professional. The resistance is a healing opportunity, not a failure. Never push away a part. All parts are welcome.

** The recording; Meditations for Self-Awareness and Self-Leadership aligns with and supports this process. To order, go to www.holisticcounselwny.com, and download more SIT Sheets for free.

Additional Notes or Parts Mapping:

Self-Inquiry Tracking (SIT) Journal Sheet   Date _____

1. Center: Focus on the flow of your breathing. Don't clear away your thoughts. Just be aware...

2. Notice: What's on your mind? List prominent thoughts/emotions/sensations. Name the part.

Thoughts ——> Emotions ——> Bodily Sensations ——> Name of Part

Ask yourself: "How do I *feel toward* this part of me?" _____
"Can I be curious, compassionate or nonjudgmental?" _____
If so, go to Step Three. If not, you have another part blocking your Self-Energy. Be inquisitive about the interference. What's it about? _____.
After listening, kindly ask the interfering part to relax and allow you to be more open and present. If the resistance won't relax, do Step Three with the resistant part. If the resistance relaxes, you can continue, focusing on the part you originally noticed.

3. Listen: In a neutral, curious way, get to know the part of you identified in Step Two. Ask whatever questions you are curious about, such as:

    a). What is your purpose (or job) within my system? _____
    b). *How* do you do your job? _____
    c). How long have you been doing this, and what is it like for you to have this job? _____
    _____
    d). What are you afraid will happen if you stop doing your job? _____
    e). What are you protecting? _____

Again, ask: "How am I feeling toward this part, now?" _____.
Tell the part. Ask other parts to soften if they interfere with your Self-Energy, e.g. compassion.

Set your intentions: Listen to your deepest impulse, and be aware of how you would authentically like to feel, if you weren't under the influence of this part. Choose the Self-Energy quality, below, that matches how you *want* to be today, in contrast to what you noticed in Step Two. Circle it below and set your intention to cultivate and hold this quality today, being aware of and manager parts that try to take over. For example: "Today I want to feel my innate confidence. I open to my confidence as the core of my being." Write your intention: _____
_____

Calm   Curiosity   Connectedness   Clarity   Compassion   Courage   Confidence   Creativity

4. Negotiate/Ask: Repeat your intention silently to your parts. Then begin leading your system of parts, asking for their cooperation:

a). Negotiate this plan by first asking the parts if they notice you and how much you care. If so, ask if they would relax, trust you, and open space for you to be Present.

They do not need to force or make this happen. They can relax while you open.

b). Be aware of (and name) any parts that resist the plan, listen to their perspectives, and keep on negotiating with them.*

5. Open/Own It: When you feel a sense of permission, get centered again by focusing on the flow of your breath, relax, and bring your fullest attention to the present moment. Find stillness. Rest there. Allow calm to arise, first. Feel your Presence. Breathe and allow your chosen quality (or others) to emerge naturally. Feel it in your body. Envision yourself being this way throughout your day. Own it. Allow it to resonate as your true, essential nature.**

Notes: _____

_____

6. Remember/Reinforce: Create a plan to remember and cultivate your chosen Self-Energy quality for today. Set alarms or reminders on your phone, naming your quality, plan pleasant activities, be aware of obstacles presented by oppositional parts. My plan for today includes:

_____

_____

Evening Reflections: How did the day go? Was I aware? What parts got triggered? Did I bring compassion-appreciation to all parts? Are there any parts who still need my attention? If so, befriend them. Notes: _____

* If you have difficulty getting beyond this point, seek support from an IFS professional. The resistance is a healing opportunity, not a failure. Never push away a part. All parts are welcome.

** The recording; Meditations for Self-Awareness and Self-Leadership aligns with and supports this process. To order, go to www.holisticcounselwny.com, and download more SIT Sheets for free.

Additional Notes or Parts Mapping:

Self-Inquiry Tracking (SIT) Journal Sheet   Date _____

1. Center: Focus on the flow of your breathing. Don't clear away your thoughts. Just be aware...

2. Notice: What's on your mind? List prominent thoughts/emotions/sensations. Name the part.

Thoughts ——> Emotions ——> Bodily Sensations ——> Name of Part

Ask yourself: "How do I *feel toward* this part of me?" _____
"Can I be curious, compassionate or nonjudgmental?" _____
If so, go to Step Three. If not, you have another part blocking your Self-Energy. Be inquisitive about the interference. What's it about? _____.
After listening, kindly ask the interfering part to relax and allow you to be more open and present. If the resistance won't relax, do Step Three with the resistant part. If the resistance relaxes, you can continue, focusing on the part you originally noticed.

3. Listen: In a neutral, curious way, get to know the part of you identified in Step Two. Ask whatever questions you are curious about, such as:
  a). What is your purpose (or job) within my system? _____
  b). *How* do you do your job? _____
  c). How long have you been doing this, and what is it like for you to have this job? _____
  d). What are you afraid will happen if you stop doing your job? _____
  e). What are you protecting? _____

Again, ask: "How am I feeling toward this part, now?" _____.
Tell the part. Ask other parts to soften if they interfere with your Self-Energy, e.g. compassion.

Set your intentions: Listen to your deepest impulse, and be aware of how you would authentically like to feel, if you weren't under the influence of this part. Choose the Self-Energy quality, below, that matches how you *want* to be today, in contrast to what you noticed in Step Two. Circle it below and set your intention to cultivate and hold this quality today, being aware of and manager parts that try to take over. For example: "Today I want to feel my innate confidence. I open to my confidence as the core of my being." Write your intention: _____
_____

Calm   Curiosity   Connectedness   Clarity   Compassion   Courage   Confidence   Creativity

4. Negotiate/Ask: Repeat your intention silently to your parts. Then begin leading your system of parts, asking for their cooperation:

    a). Negotiate this plan by first asking the parts if they notice you and how much you care. If so, ask if they would relax, trust you, and open space for you to be Present.

        They do not need to force or make this happen. They can relax while you open.

    b). Be aware of (and name) any parts that resist the plan, listen to their perspectives, and keep on negotiating with them.*

5. Open/Own It: When you feel a sense of permission, get centered again by focusing on the flow of your breath, relax, and bring your fullest attention to the present moment. Find stillness. Rest there. Allow calm to arise, first. Feel your Presence. Breathe and allow your chosen quality (or others) to emerge naturally. Feel it in your body. Envision yourself being this way throughout your day. Own it. Allow it to resonate as your true, essential nature.**

Notes: _____

_____

6. Remember/Reinforce: Create a plan to remember and cultivate your chosen Self-Energy quality for today. Set alarms or reminders on your phone, naming your quality, plan pleasant activities, be aware of obstacles presented by oppositional parts. My plan for today includes:

_____

_____

Evening Reflections: How did the day go? Was I aware? What parts got triggered? Did I bring compassion-appreciation to all parts? Are there any parts who still need my attention? If so, befriend them. Notes: _____

* If you have difficulty getting beyond this point, seek support from an IFS professional. The resistance is a healing opportunity, not a failure. Never push away a part. All parts are welcome.

** The recording; Meditations for Self-Awareness and Self-Leadership aligns with and supports this process. To order, go to www.holisticcounselwny.com, and download more SIT Sheets for free.

Additional Notes or Parts Mapping:

Self-Inquiry Tracking (SIT) Journal Sheet   Date _____

1. Center: Focus on the flow of your breathing. Don't clear away your thoughts. Just be aware...

2. Notice: What's on your mind? List prominent thoughts/emotions/sensations. Name the part.

Thoughts   ——>   Emotions   ——>   Bodily Sensations   ——>   Name of Part

Ask yourself: "How do I *feel toward* this part of me?" _____
"Can I be curious, compassionate or nonjudgmental?" _____
If so, go to Step Three. If not, you have another part blocking your Self-Energy. Be inquisitive about the interference. What's it about? _____.
After listening, kindly ask the interfering part to relax and allow you to be more open and present. If the resistance won't relax, do Step Three with the resistant part. If the resistance relaxes, you can continue, focusing on the part you originally noticed.

3. Listen: In a neutral, curious way, get to know the part of you identified in Step Two. Ask whatever questions you are curious about, such as:

   a). What is your purpose (or job) within my system? _____
   b). *How* do you do your job? _____
   c). How long have you been doing this, and what is it like for you to have this job? _____
   _____
   d). What are you afraid will happen if you stop doing your job? _____
   e). What are you protecting? _____

Again, ask: "How am I feeling toward this part, now?" _____.
Tell the part. Ask other parts to soften if they interfere with your Self-Energy, e.g. compassion.

Set your intentions: Listen to your deepest impulse, and be aware of how you would authentically like to feel, if you weren't under the influence of this part. Choose the Self-Energy quality, below, that matches how you *want* to be today, in contrast to what you noticed in Step Two. Circle it below and set your intention to cultivate and hold this quality today, being aware of and manager parts that try to take over. For example: "Today I want to feel my innate confidence. I open to my confidence as the core of my being." Write your intention: _____
_____

Calm   Curiosity   Connectedness   Clarity   Compassion   Courage   Confidence   Creativity

4. Negotiate/Ask: Repeat your intention silently to your parts. Then begin leading your system of parts, asking for their cooperation:

a). Negotiate this plan by first asking the parts if they notice you and how much you care. If so, ask if they would relax, trust you, and open space for you to be Present.

They do not need to force or make this happen. They can relax while you open.

b). Be aware of (and name) any parts that resist the plan, listen to their perspectives, and keep on negotiating with them.*

5. Open/Own It: When you feel a sense of permission, get centered again by focusing on the flow of your breath, relax, and bring your fullest attention to the present moment. Find stillness. Rest there. Allow calm to arise, first. Feel your Presence. Breathe and allow your chosen quality (or others) to emerge naturally. Feel it in your body. Envision yourself being this way throughout your day. Own it. Allow it to resonate as your true, essential nature.**
Notes: _____
_____

6. Remember/Reinforce: Create a plan to remember and cultivate your chosen Self-Energy quality for today. Set alarms or reminders on your phone, naming your quality, plan pleasant activities, be aware of obstacles presented by oppositional parts. My plan for today includes:
_____
_____

Evening Reflections: How did the day go? Was I aware? What parts got triggered? Did I bring compassion-appreciation to all parts? Are there any parts who still need my attention? If so, befriend them. Notes: _____

* If you have difficulty getting beyond this point, seek support from an IFS professional. The resistance is a healing opportunity, not a failure. Never push away a part. All parts are welcome.

** The recording; Meditations for Self-Awareness and Self-Leadership aligns with and supports this process. To order, go to www.holisticcounselwny.com, and download more SIT Sheets for free.

Additional Notes or Parts Mapping:

Self-Inquiry Tracking (SIT) Journal Sheet   Date _____

1. Center: Focus on the flow of your breathing. Don't clear away your thoughts. Just be aware…

2. Notice: What's on your mind? List prominent thoughts/emotions/sensations. Name the part.

Thoughts   ——>   Emotions   ——>   Bodily Sensations   ——>   Name of Part

Ask yourself: "How do I *feel toward* this part of me?" _____
"Can I be curious, compassionate or nonjudgmental?" _____
If so, go to Step Three. If not, you have another part blocking your Self-Energy. Be inquisitive about the interference. What's it about? _____.
After listening, kindly ask the interfering part to relax and allow you to be more open and present. If the resistance won't relax, do Step Three with the resistant part. If the resistance relaxes, you can continue, focusing on the part you originally noticed.

3. Listen: In a neutral, curious way, get to know the part of you identified in Step Two. Ask whatever questions you are curious about, such as:
    a). What is your purpose (or job) within my system? _____
    b). *How* do you do your job? _____
    c). How long have you been doing this, and what is it like for you to have this job? _____
    _____
    d). What are you afraid will happen if you stop doing your job? _____
    e). What are you protecting? _____

Again, ask: "How am I feeling toward this part, now?" _____.
Tell the part. Ask other parts to soften if they interfere with your Self-Energy, e.g. compassion.

Set your intentions: Listen to your deepest impulse, and be aware of how you would authentically like to feel, if you weren't under the influence of this part. Choose the Self-Energy quality, below, that matches how you *want* to be today, in contrast to what you noticed in Step Two. Circle it below and set your intention to cultivate and hold this quality today, being aware of and manager parts that try to take over. For example: "Today I want to feel my innate confidence. I open to my confidence as the core of my being." Write your intention: _____
_____

Calm   *Curiosity*   *Connectedness*   *Clarity*   *Compassion*   *Courage*   *Confidence*   *Creativity*

4. Negotiate/Ask: Repeat your intention silently to your parts. Then begin leading your system of parts, asking for their cooperation:

    a). Negotiate this plan by first asking the parts if they notice you and how much you care. If so, ask if they would relax, trust you, and open space for you to be Present.

        They do not need to force or make this happen. They can relax while you open.

    b). Be aware of (and name) any parts that resist the plan, listen to their perspectives, and keep on negotiating with them.*

5. Open/Own It: When you feel a sense of permission, get centered again by focusing on the flow of your breath, relax, and bring your fullest attention to the present moment. Find stillness. Rest there. Allow calm to arise, first. Feel your Presence. Breathe and allow your chosen quality (or others) to emerge naturally. Feel it in your body. Envision yourself being this way throughout your day. Own it. Allow it to resonate as your true, essential nature.**

Notes: _____

_____

6. Remember/Reinforce: Create a plan to remember and cultivate your chosen Self-Energy quality for today. Set alarms or reminders on your phone, naming your quality, plan pleasant activities, be aware of obstacles presented by oppositional parts. My plan for today includes:

_____

_____

Evening Reflections: How did the day go? Was I aware? What parts got triggered? Did I bring compassion-appreciation to all parts? Are there any parts who still need my attention? If so, befriend them. Notes: _____

* If you have difficulty getting beyond this point, seek support from an IFS professional. The resistance is a healing opportunity, not a failure. Never push away a part. All parts are welcome.

** The recording; Meditations for Self-Awareness and Self-Leadership aligns with and supports this process. To order, go to www.holisticcounselwny.com, and download more SIT Sheets for free.

Additional Notes or Parts Mapping:

Self-Inquiry Tracking (SIT) Journal Sheet   Date _____

1. Center: Focus on the flow of your breathing. Don't clear away your thoughts. Just be aware...

2. Notice: What's on your mind? List prominent thoughts/emotions/sensations. Name the part.

Thoughts ——> Emotions ——> Bodily Sensations ——> Name of Part

Ask yourself: "How do I *feel toward* this part of me?" _____
"Can I be curious, compassionate or nonjudgmental?" _____
If so, go to Step Three. If not, you have another part blocking your Self-Energy. Be inquisitive about the interference. What's it about? _____.
After listening, kindly ask the interfering part to relax and allow you to be more open and present. If the resistance won't relax, do Step Three with the resistant part. If the resistance relaxes, you can continue, focusing on the part you originally noticed.

3. Listen: In a neutral, curious way, get to know the part of you identified in Step Two. Ask whatever questions you are curious about, such as:

   a). What is your purpose (or job) within my system? _____
   b). *How* do you do your job? _____
   c). How long have you been doing this, and what is it like for you to have this job? _____
   _____
   d). What are you afraid will happen if you stop doing your job? _____
   e). What are you protecting? _____

Again, ask: "How am I feeling toward this part, now?" _____.
Tell the part. Ask other parts to soften if they interfere with your Self-Energy, e.g. compassion.

Set your intentions: Listen to your deepest impulse, and be aware of how you would authentically like to feel, if you weren't under the influence of this part. Choose the Self-Energy quality, below, that matches how you *want* to be today, in contrast to what you noticed in Step Two. Circle it below and set your intention to cultivate and hold this quality today, being aware of and manager parts that try to take over. For example: "Today I want to feel my innate confidence. I open to my confidence as the core of my being." Write your intention: _____
_____

Calm   Curiosity   Connectedness   Clarity   Compassion   Courage   Confidence   Creativity

4. Negotiate/Ask: Repeat your intention silently to your parts. Then begin leading your system of parts, asking for their cooperation:

    a). Negotiate this plan by first asking the parts if they notice you and how much you care. If so, ask if they would relax, trust you, and open space for you to be Present.

        They do not need to force or make this happen. They can relax while you open.

    b). Be aware of (and name) any parts that resist the plan, listen to their perspectives, and keep on negotiating with them.*

5. Open/Own It: When you feel a sense of permission, get centered again by focusing on the flow of your breath, relax, and bring your fullest attention to the present moment. Find stillness. Rest there. Allow calm to arise, first. Feel your Presence. Breathe and allow your chosen quality (or others) to emerge naturally. Feel it in your body. Envision yourself being this way throughout your day. Own it. Allow it to resonate as your true, essential nature.**

Notes: _____

_____

6. Remember/Reinforce: Create a plan to remember and cultivate your chosen Self-Energy quality for today. Set alarms or reminders on your phone, naming your quality, plan pleasant activities, be aware of obstacles presented by oppositional parts. My plan for today includes:

_____

_____

Evening Reflections: How did the day go? Was I aware? What parts got triggered? Did I bring compassion-appreciation to all parts? Are there any parts who still need my attention? If so, befriend them. Notes: _____

* If you have difficulty getting beyond this point, seek support from an IFS professional. The resistance is a healing opportunity, not a failure. Never push away a part. All parts are welcome.

** The recording; Meditations for Self-Awareness and Self-Leadership aligns with and supports this process. To order, go to www.holisticcounselwny.com, and download more SIT Sheets for free.

Additional Notes or Parts Mapping:

Self-Inquiry Tracking (SIT) Journal Sheet   Date _____

1. Center: Focus on the flow of your breathing. Don't clear away your thoughts. Just be aware…

2. Notice: What's on your mind? List prominent thoughts/emotions/sensations. Name the part.

Thoughts ——> Emotions ——> Bodily Sensations ——> Name of Part

Ask yourself: "How do I *feel toward* this part of me?" _____
"Can I be curious, compassionate or nonjudgmental?" _____
If so, go to Step Three. If not, you have another part blocking your Self-Energy. Be inquisitive about the interference. What's it about? _____.
After listening, kindly ask the interfering part to relax and allow you to be more open and present. If the resistance won't relax, do Step Three with the resistant part. If the resistance relaxes, you can continue, focusing on the part you originally noticed.

3. Listen: In a neutral, curious way, get to know the part of you identified in Step Two. Ask whatever questions you are curious about, such as:
   a). What is your purpose (or job) within my system? _____
   b). *How* do you do your job? _____
   c). How long have you been doing this, and what is it like for you to have this job? _____
   _____
   d). What are you afraid will happen if you stop doing your job? _____
   e). What are you protecting? _____

Again, ask: "How am I feeling toward this part, now?" _____.
Tell the part. Ask other parts to soften if they interfere with your Self-Energy, e.g. compassion.

Set your intentions: Listen to your deepest impulse, and be aware of how you would authentically like to feel, if you weren't under the influence of this part. Choose the Self-Energy quality, below, that matches how you *want* to be today, in contrast to what you noticed in Step Two. Circle it below and set your intention to cultivate and hold this quality today, being aware of and manager parts that try to take over. For example: "Today I want to feel my innate confidence. I open to my confidence as the core of my being." Write your intention: _____
_____

Calm   Curiosity   Connectedness   Clarity   Compassion   Courage   Confidence   Creativity

4. Negotiate/Ask: Repeat your intention silently to your parts. Then begin leading your system of parts, asking for their cooperation:

   a). Negotiate this plan by first asking the parts if they notice you and how much you care. If so, ask if they would relax, trust you, and open space for you to be Present.

   They do not need to force or make this happen. They can relax while you open.

   b). Be aware of (and name) any parts that resist the plan, listen to their perspectives, and keep on negotiating with them.*

5. Open/Own It: When you feel a sense of permission, get centered again by focusing on the flow of your breath, relax, and bring your fullest attention to the present moment. Find stillness. Rest there. Allow calm to arise, first. Feel your Presence. Breathe and allow your chosen quality (or others) to emerge naturally. Feel it in your body. Envision yourself being this way throughout your day. Own it. Allow it to resonate as your true, essential nature.**

Notes: _____

_____

6. Remember/Reinforce: Create a plan to remember and cultivate your chosen Self-Energy quality for today. Set alarms or reminders on your phone, naming your quality, plan pleasant activities, be aware of obstacles presented by oppositional parts. My plan for today includes:

_____

_____

Evening Reflections: How did the day go? Was I aware? What parts got triggered? Did I bring compassion-appreciation to all parts? Are there any parts who still need my attention? If so, befriend them. Notes: _____

* If you have difficulty getting beyond this point, seek support from an IFS professional. The resistance is a healing opportunity, not a failure. Never push away a part. All parts are welcome.

** The recording; Meditations for Self-Awareness and Self-Leadership aligns with and supports this process. To order, go to www.holisticcounselwny.com, and download more SIT Sheets for free.

Additional Notes or Parts Mapping:

Self-Inquiry Tracking (SIT) Journal Sheet   Date _____

1. Center: Focus on the flow of your breathing. Don't clear away your thoughts. Just be aware...

2. Notice: What's on your mind? List prominent thoughts/emotions/sensations. Name the part.

Thoughts   ——>   Emotions   ——>   Bodily Sensations   ——>   Name of Part

Ask yourself: "How do I *feel toward* this part of me?" _____
"Can I be curious, compassionate or nonjudgmental?" _____
If so, go to Step Three. If not, you have another part blocking your Self-Energy. Be inquisitive about the interference. What's it about? _____.
After listening, kindly ask the interfering part to relax and allow you to be more open and present. If the resistance won't relax, do Step Three with the resistant part. If the resistance relaxes, you can continue, focusing on the part you originally noticed.

3. Listen: In a neutral, curious way, get to know the part of you identified in Step Two. Ask whatever questions you are curious about, such as:

  a). What is your purpose (or job) within my system? _____
  b). *How* do you do your job? _____
  c). How long have you been doing this, and what is it like for you to have this job? _____
  _____
  d). What are you afraid will happen if you stop doing your job? _____
  e). What are you protecting? _____

Again, ask: "How am I feeling toward this part, now?" _____.
Tell the part. Ask other parts to soften if they interfere with your Self-Energy, e.g. compassion.

Set your intentions: Listen to your deepest impulse, and be aware of how you would authentically like to feel, if you weren't under the influence of this part. Choose the Self-Energy quality, below, that matches how you *want* to be today, in contrast to what you noticed in Step Two. Circle it below and set your intention to cultivate and hold this quality today, being aware of and manager parts that try to take over. For example: "Today I want to feel my innate confidence. I open to my confidence as the core of my being." Write your intention: _____
_____

Calm   Curiosity   Connectedness   Clarity   Compassion   Courage   Confidence   Creativity

4. Negotiate/Ask: Repeat your intention silently to your parts. Then begin leading your system of parts, asking for their cooperation:

a). Negotiate this plan by first asking the parts if they notice you and how much you care. If so, ask if they would relax, trust you, and open space for you to be Present.

They do not need to force or make this happen. They can relax while you open.

b). Be aware of (and name) any parts that resist the plan, listen to their perspectives, and keep on negotiating with them.*

5. Open/Own It: When you feel a sense of permission, get centered again by focusing on the flow of your breath, relax, and bring your fullest attention to the present moment. Find stillness. Rest there. Allow calm to arise, first. Feel your Presence. Breathe and allow your chosen quality (or others) to emerge naturally. Feel it in your body. Envision yourself being this way throughout your day. Own it. Allow it to resonate as your true, essential nature.**

Notes: _____

_____

6. Remember/Reinforce: Create a plan to remember and cultivate your chosen Self-Energy quality for today. Set alarms or reminders on your phone, naming your quality, plan pleasant activities, be aware of obstacles presented by oppositional parts. My plan for today includes:

_____

_____

Evening Reflections: How did the day go? Was I aware? What parts got triggered? Did I bring compassion-appreciation to all parts? Are there any parts who still need my attention? If so, befriend them. Notes: _____

* If you have difficulty getting beyond this point, seek support from an IFS professional. The resistance is a healing opportunity, not a failure. Never push away a part. All parts are welcome.

** The recording; Meditations for Self-Awareness and Self-Leadership aligns with and supports this process. To order, go to www.holisticcounselwny.com, and download more SIT Sheets for free.

Additional Notes or Parts Mapping:

Self-Inquiry Tracking (SIT) Journal Sheet   Date _____

1. Center: Focus on the flow of your breathing. Don't clear away your thoughts. Just be aware…

2. Notice: What's on your mind? List prominent thoughts/emotions/sensations. Name the part.

Thoughts   ——>   Emotions   ——>   Bodily Sensations   ——>   Name of Part

Ask yourself: "How do I *feel toward* this part of me?" _____
"Can I be curious, compassionate or nonjudgmental?" _____
If so, go to Step Three. If not, you have another part blocking your Self-Energy. Be inquisitive about the interference. What's it about? _____.
After listening, kindly ask the interfering part to relax and allow you to be more open and present. If the resistance won't relax, do Step Three with the resistant part. If the resistance relaxes, you can continue, focusing on the part you originally noticed.

3. Listen: In a neutral, curious way, get to know the part of you identified in Step Two. Ask whatever questions you are curious about, such as:
   a). What is your purpose (or job) within my system? _____
   b). *How* do you do your job? _____
   c). How long have you been doing this, and what is it like for you to have this job? _____
   _____
   d). What are you afraid will happen if you stop doing your job? _____
   e). What are you protecting? _____

Again, ask: "How am I feeling toward this part, now?" _____.
Tell the part. Ask other parts to soften if they interfere with your Self-Energy, e.g. compassion.

Set your intentions: Listen to your deepest impulse, and be aware of how you would authentically like to feel, if you weren't under the influence of this part. Choose the Self-Energy quality, below, that matches how you *want* to be today, in contrast to what you noticed in Step Two. Circle it below and set your intention to cultivate and hold this quality today, being aware of and manager parts that try to take over. For example: "Today I want to feel my innate confidence. I open to my confidence as the core of my being." Write your intention: _____
_____

Calm   Curiosity   Connectedness   Clarity   Compassion   Courage   Confidence   Creativity

4. Negotiate/Ask: Repeat your intention silently to your parts. Then begin leading your system of parts, asking for their cooperation:

    a). Negotiate this plan by first asking the parts if they notice you and how much you care. If so, ask if they would relax, trust you, and open space for you to be Present.

        They do not need to force or make this happen. They can relax while you open.

    b). Be aware of (and name) any parts that resist the plan, listen to their perspectives, and keep on negotiating with them.*

5. Open/Own It: When you feel a sense of permission, get centered again by focusing on the flow of your breath, relax, and bring your fullest attention to the present moment. Find stillness. Rest there. Allow calm to arise, first. Feel your Presence. Breathe and allow your chosen quality (or others) to emerge naturally. Feel it in your body. Envision yourself being this way throughout your day. Own it. Allow it to resonate as your true, essential nature.**

Notes: _____

_____

6. Remember/Reinforce: Create a plan to remember and cultivate your chosen Self-Energy quality for today. Set alarms or reminders on your phone, naming your quality, plan pleasant activities, be aware of obstacles presented by oppositional parts. My plan for today includes:

_____

_____

Evening Reflections: How did the day go? Was I aware? What parts got triggered? Did I bring compassion-appreciation to all parts? Are there any parts who still need my attention? If so, befriend them. Notes: _____

* If you have difficulty getting beyond this point, seek support from an IFS professional. The resistance is a healing opportunity, not a failure. Never push away a part. All parts are welcome.

** The recording; Meditations for Self-Awareness and Self-Leadership aligns with and supports this process. To order, go to www.holisticcounselwny.com, and download more SIT Sheets for free.

Additional Notes or Parts Mapping:

Self-Inquiry Tracking (SIT) Journal Sheet   Date _____

1. Center: Focus on the flow of your breathing. Don't clear away your thoughts. Just be aware...

2. Notice: What's on your mind? List prominent thoughts/emotions/sensations. Name the part.

Thoughts ——> Emotions ——> Bodily Sensations ——> Name of Part

Ask yourself: "How do I *feel toward* this part of me?" _____
"Can I be curious, compassionate or nonjudgmental?" _____
If so, go to Step Three. If not, you have another part blocking your Self-Energy. Be inquisitive about the interference. What's it about? _____.
After listening, kindly ask the interfering part to relax and allow you to be more open and present. If the resistance won't relax, do Step Three with the resistant part. If the resistance relaxes, you can continue, focusing on the part you originally noticed.

3. Listen: In a neutral, curious way, get to know the part of you identified in Step Two. Ask whatever questions you are curious about, such as:

   a). What is your purpose (or job) within my system? _____
   b). *How* do you do your job? _____
   c). How long have you been doing this, and what is it like for you to have this job? _____
   _____
   d). What are you afraid will happen if you stop doing your job? _____
   e). What are you protecting? _____

Again, ask: "How am I feeling toward this part, now?" _____.
Tell the part. Ask other parts to soften if they interfere with your Self-Energy, e.g. compassion.

Set your intentions: Listen to your deepest impulse, and be aware of how you would authentically like to feel, if you weren't under the influence of this part. Choose the Self-Energy quality, below, that matches how you *want* to be today, in contrast to what you noticed in Step Two. Circle it below and set your intention to cultivate and hold this quality today, being aware of and manager parts that try to take over. For example: "Today I want to feel my innate confidence. I open to my confidence as the core of my being." Write your intention: _____
_____

Calm   Curiosity   Connectedness   Clarity   Compassion   Courage   Confidence   Creativity

4. Negotiate/Ask: Repeat your intention silently to your parts. Then begin leading your system of parts, asking for their cooperation:

a). Negotiate this plan by first asking the parts if they notice you and how much you care. If so, ask if they would relax, trust you, and open space for you to be Present.

They do not need to force or make this happen. They can relax while you open.

b). Be aware of (and name) any parts that resist the plan, listen to their perspectives, and keep on negotiating with them.*

5. Open/Own It: When you feel a sense of permission, get centered again by focusing on the flow of your breath, relax, and bring your fullest attention to the present moment. Find stillness. Rest there. Allow calm to arise, first. Feel your Presence. Breathe and allow your chosen quality (or others) to emerge naturally. Feel it in your body. Envision yourself being this way throughout your day. Own it. Allow it to resonate as your true, essential nature.**
Notes: _____
_____

6. Remember/Reinforce: Create a plan to remember and cultivate your chosen Self-Energy quality for today. Set alarms or reminders on your phone, naming your quality, plan pleasant activities, be aware of obstacles presented by oppositional parts. My plan for today includes:
_____
_____

Evening Reflections: How did the day go? Was I aware? What parts got triggered? Did I bring compassion-appreciation to all parts? Are there any parts who still need my attention? If so, befriend them. Notes: _____

* If you have difficulty getting beyond this point, seek support from an IFS professional. The resistance is a healing opportunity, not a failure. Never push away a part. All parts are welcome.

** The recording; Meditations for Self-Awareness and Self-Leadership aligns with and supports this process. To order, go to www.holisticcounselwny.com, and download more SIT Sheets for free.

Additional Notes or Parts Mapping:

Self-Inquiry Tracking (SIT) Journal Sheet   Date _____

1. Center: Focus on the flow of your breathing. Don't clear away your thoughts. Just be aware…

2. Notice: What's on your mind? List prominent thoughts/emotions/sensations. Name the part.

Thoughts ——> Emotions ——> Bodily Sensations ——> Name of Part

Ask yourself: "How do I *feel toward* this part of me?" _____
"Can I be curious, compassionate or nonjudgmental?" _____
If so, go to Step Three. If not, you have another part blocking your Self-Energy. Be inquisitive about the interference. What's it about? _____.
After listening, kindly ask the interfering part to relax and allow you to be more open and present. If the resistance won't relax, do Step Three with the resistant part. If the resistance relaxes, you can continue, focusing on the part you originally noticed.

3. Listen: In a neutral, curious way, get to know the part of you identified in Step Two. Ask whatever questions you are curious about, such as:

   a). What is your purpose (or job) within my system? _____
   b). *How* do you do your job? _____
   c). How long have you been doing this, and what is it like for you to have this job? _____
   _____
   d). What are you afraid will happen if you stop doing your job? _____
   e). What are you protecting? _____

Again, ask: "How am I feeling toward this part, now?" _____.
Tell the part. Ask other parts to soften if they interfere with your Self-Energy, e.g. compassion.

Set your intentions: Listen to your deepest impulse, and be aware of how you would authentically like to feel, if you weren't under the influence of this part. Choose the Self-Energy quality, below, that matches how you *want* to be today, in contrast to what you noticed in Step Two. Circle it below and set your intention to cultivate and hold this quality today, being aware of and manager parts that try to take over. For example: "Today I want to feel my innate confidence. I open to my confidence as the core of my being." Write your intention: _____
_____

Calm   Curiosity   Connectedness   Clarity   Compassion   Courage   Confidence   Creativity

4. Negotiate/Ask: Repeat your intention silently to your parts. Then begin leading your system of parts, asking for their cooperation:

    a). Negotiate this plan by first asking the parts if they notice you and how much you care. If so, ask if they would relax, trust you, and open space for you to be Present.

        They do not need to force or make this happen. They can relax while you open.

    b). Be aware of (and name) any parts that resist the plan, listen to their perspectives, and keep on negotiating with them.*

5. Open/Own It: When you feel a sense of permission, get centered again by focusing on the flow of your breath, relax, and bring your fullest attention to the present moment. Find stillness. Rest there. Allow calm to arise, first. Feel your Presence. Breathe and allow your chosen quality (or others) to emerge naturally. Feel it in your body. Envision yourself being this way throughout your day. Own it. Allow it to resonate as your true, essential nature.**

Notes: _____

_____

6. Remember/Reinforce: Create a plan to remember and cultivate your chosen Self-Energy quality for today. Set alarms or reminders on your phone, naming your quality, plan pleasant activities, be aware of obstacles presented by oppositional parts. My plan for today includes:

_____

_____

Evening Reflections: How did the day go? Was I aware? What parts got triggered? Did I bring compassion-appreciation to all parts? Are there any parts who still need my attention? If so, befriend them. Notes: _____

* If you have difficulty getting beyond this point, seek support from an IFS professional. The resistance is a healing opportunity, not a failure. Never push away a part. All parts are welcome.

** The recording; Meditations for Self-Awareness and Self-Leadership aligns with and supports this process. To order, go to www.holisticcounselwny.com, and download more SIT Sheets for free.

Additional Notes or Parts Mapping:

www.ingramcontent.com/pod-product-compliance
Lightning Source LLC
Chambersburg PA
CBHW081840170426
43199CB00017B/2796